CREATING
ETHNICITY

FRONTIERS OF ANTHROPOLOGY

Series Editor:

H. RUSSELL BERNARD, *University of Florida*

The **Frontiers of Anthropology** series is designed to explore the leading edge of theory, method, and applications in cultural anthropology. In rapidly changing times, traditional ways in which anthropologists work have been transformed, being influenced by new paradigms, methodological approaches beyond the use of participant observation, and field settings beyond the world of primitive peoples. Books in this series come from many philosophical schools, methodological approaches, substantive concerns, and geographical settings—some familiar to anthropologists and some new to the discipline. But all share the purpose of examining and explaining the ideas and practices that make up the frontiers of contemporary cultural anthropology.

Books in This Series

FAMILY VIOLENCE IN CROSS-CULTURAL PERSPECTIVE
by **DAVID LEVINSON**, *Vice President*
Human Relations Area Files, New Haven
Frontiers of Anthropology, Volume 1
ISBN: 0-8039-3075-5 (cloth) ISBN: 0-8039-3076-3 (paper)

WOMEN'S POWER AND SOCIAL REVOLUTION
Fertility Transition in the West Indies
by **W. PENN HANDWERKER**, *Humboldt State University*
Frontiers of Anthropology, Volume 2
ISBN: 0-8039-3115-8 (cloth) ISBN: 0-8039-3116-6 (paper)

WAREHOUSING VIOLENCE
by **MARK S. FLEISHER**, *Washington State University*
Frontiers of Anthropology, Volume 3
ISBN: 0-8039-3122-0 (cloth) ISBN: 0-8039-3123-9 (paper)

CAPITAL CRIME
Black Infant Mortality in America
by **MARGARET S. BOONE**, *George Washington University,*
School of Medicine and Health Sciences
Frontiers of Anthropology, Volume 4
ISBN: 0-8039-3373-8 (cloth) ISBN: 0-8039-3374-6 (paper)

CREATING ETHNICITY
The Process of Ethnogenesis
by **EUGEEN E. ROOSENS**, *Catholic University of Leuven*
Frontiers of Anthropology, Volume 5
ISBN: 0-8039-3422-X (cloth) ISBN: 0-8039-3423-8 (paper)

INTERNATIONAL HUMAN RIGHTS
Universalism Versus Relativism
by **ALISON DUNDES RENTELN**, *University of Southern California*
Frontiers of Anthropology, Volume 6
ISBN: 0-8039-3505-6 (cloth) ISBN: 0-8039-3506-4 (paper)

CREATING ETHNICITY

The Process of Ethnogenesis

EUGEEN E. ROOSENS

Frontiers of Anthropology   Volume 5

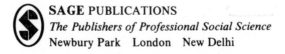

SAGE PUBLICATIONS
The Publishers of Professional Social Science
Newbury Park   London   New Delhi

To Johanna

For information address:

SAGE Publications, Inc.
2111 West Hillcrest Drive
Newbury Park, California 91320

SAGE Publications Ltd.
28 Banner Street
London EC1Y 8QE
England

SAGE Publications India Pvt. Ltd.
M-32 Market
Greater Kailash I
New Delhi 110 048 India

Printed in the United States of America

Library of Congress Cataloguing-in-Publication Data

Roosens, Eugeen, 1934-
  Creating ethnicity : the process of ethnogenesis / Eugeen E.
Roosens.
      p.   cm. — (Frontiers of anthropology ; v. 5)
      Bibliography: p.
      ISBN 0-8039-3422-X. — ISBN 0-8039-3423-8 (pbk.)
      1. Ethnicity. 2. Ethnic groups.   I. Title.   II. Series.
  GN495.6.R66   1990
  305.8—dc20   89-10549
                                                                       CIP

FIRST PRINTING, 1989

Contents

Acknowledgments   8

**1 The Making of Natural Feelings: Problems, Concepts,
   and Theoretical Starting Point**   **9**
   Ethnicity: A Worldwide Phenomenon   9
   Research and Case Studies   10
   Theoretical Starting Point   11
     The Concept of "Ethnic Group"   12
       Ethnic Group and Observable Culture   12
       Self-Ascribed Culture and Social Boundaries   12
     Ethnicity and Economic Interest   13
     Ethnic Groups: Pressure Groups with a Noble Face   14
     Ethnic Identity: A Psychological Reality   15
     The 1960s and 1970s: A Propitious Time for Ethnicity   17
     The Flexibility of Ethnic Identification   17
     Political Manipulation   18
     The Many Faces of Ethnicity   19

2 Indian Status   **21**
   The Indians, Canada, and Quebec   21
   Who Is an Indian? "Nature" and Ethnic Engineering   23
   The Historical Development of Indian Status: Ethnic
     Definitions as a Tool of Extinction   25
   The Ethnic "Mutation" of Women: An Unfair Deal   30
   "Nature" Bounces Back   32
   The Logical Muddles of Ethnic Engineering   34
   Who Is Who? A Power Struggle   37
   The Cultural Nature of Biological Descent   41
   The Indian Law: Backfiring Factitiousness   43

3 The Hurons of Quebec   **45**
   The Huron Village in 1968: A Nascent Counterculture   45
   A Historian's Viewpoint   47
   A United Front   57
   Splitting   57

4 Indian Political Ideology and Harder Facts   **61**
   The Viewpoint of a Political Leader   61
     In Search of the Truth   61
     Political Inspiration   62
     The "Natural" Superiority of the "First Cultures"   62
     The Avid Openness of Indian Culture   65

"The Archaic Illusion"   65
Ethnic Logic: Horizontal Equality   67
The Socioeconomic Conditions of the Indians: Undeniable Facts   68
   The Fate of Downtrodden Nations: Marginal Dependency   69
   The World of White Goods: A Fatal Temptation   70
   Cultural Incongruities   71
   The Bypass Fallacy   71
   The Practical Limits of Cultural Relativity   72
   Rhetoric and Facts   73

5 **"French" Expertise and "French" Autochthony**   **75**
   The Dorion Commission   75
      Indian Rights: Some Evidence   75
      A "French" Point of View: The Power of the Written Text   77
      Ethnocentric Expertise   78
   The Parti Québecois   79
      The "French" as Colonized American Aborigines   79
      Swallowing the Preaborigines   82

6 **Closer to Reality: Conversations with Huron Citizens**   **85**
   The Feeling of Being a Downtrodden, Vanishing Nation   85
   The Indestructable Nature of Ethnic Belonging   88
   The Feeling of Dying Out   89
   Modern Tools for Traditional Survival   91
   Indian Traits and Ethnic Feelings: Culture and Ethnicity   96
   The Cultural Foundation of Huron Ethnicity   96

7 **The Aymara of Turco: Hurons in Reverse**   **103**
   Turco in Bolivia   103
   Fighting Tradition and Ethnicity from the Inside   105
   Superior Modernity   106
   The Futility of Being a Native   107
   Passing   108
   Holy Temptation: The World of Catholic Goods   108
   The "Savages" of the Aymara: Ethnicity in the Past   110
   "Unethnic" Continuities with the Past   112
   The Aymara and the Hurons: The Unifying Power of
      Practical Reason   113

8 **The Luba of Kasai (Zaire): New "White" Ethnics**   **117**
   Preethnic "Natives"   117
   The Historical Growth of Ethnicity   119
   Theoretical Reflections   122

9   Ethnic Minorities in Belgium: Among Potential Equals   127
Belgium: A Multiethnic Society, Whether It Wants to Be or Not   127
Native Communities: Ethnic Splitting as a Fashionable Trend   128
   A False Picture of the Ethnic Past   128
   Ethnogenesis: A Process Growing over the Years   129
   "Strangers": A Clear-Cut Category   129
   A Recent Distinction: EEC-Strangers and the Others   130
The First Generation: "Natural" Ethnics   132
   A Useful Underclass   132
   "Nouveaux Riches" in the Home Country   133
   Ethnic Continuity: A Rewarding Form of Identification   134
   The Unifying Process of Material Production   135
   Cultural Emblems of Ethnic Belonging   136
   "Domestic Foreigners"   136
The Second Generation   137
   Cultural Assimilation   137
   Social Isolation   138
   Psychosocial Return to the Ethnic Group   139
Trying to Shape a "Multicultural Society"   142
   The "Migrant Question" in Brussels: An Explosive Issue   142
   The Complexity of Organizing Bicultural or Multicultural
     Education   142
   A State-Subsidized Muslim Educational Network?   144
   The Danger of Apartheid   144
   Broadening the Experimental Phase in Bicultural Education   145
   Bi- and Trilingualism: A Considerable Asset   146
Emerging Europe: Ethnic Relations of an Original Nature   147

10   Final Reflections: Ethnic Subtleties   149
Ethnic Identity in Plural Form   149
Ethnic Struggle in Cultural Form: Conditions   150
   Ethnicity, Acculturation, and Power Relationships   150
   Cultural Relativism as a Perspective of the Actor   152
   "Culture": A Useful Weapon in Peaceful Settings   153
   "Culture Struggle": A Problem of Wealthy States   153
   Culture and Power   154
Strategic Advantages of Cultural Identity in Ethnic Relations   154
   The Prehensile Openness of Culture   154
   The Elasticity of Culture and History   155
The Objective Core of Human Construction   156
Ethnicity and Modern Material Resources: Dialectical Change   156
   Ethnic Differentiation and Growing Cultural Uniformity   157
   Ethnicity and Social Equalization   158
Ethnicity and the Creation of "Natural" Symbols   159

References   163

About the Author   168

Acknowledgments

The Conseil des arts du Canada, the Ford Foundation, the Belgian National Fund for Scientific Research, and the Research Fund of the Catholic University of Leuven have sponsored the research on which this book is based. I am much indebted to these institutions.

I would also like to express my gratitude to the citizens of Huron Village and their Grand Chief, Max Gros-Louis. The collaboration of my good friend François Vincent of Huron Village has been very much appreciated throughout the years.

I thank, too, the editors of Academisch Coöperatief (Leuven/Amersfoort), who have published major portions of this book in Dutch.

I am most indebted to Professor H. Russell Bernard for making numerous valuable comments on the drafts and for rewriting the English version of the text.

— Eugeen E. Roosens

-1-

THE MAKING OF NATURAL FEELINGS

Problems, Concepts, and Theoretical Starting Point

ETHNICITY: A WORLDWIDE PHENOMENON

Twenty-five years ago, researchers of culture change generally assumed that direct and continuous contact between groups of different cultures would lead to a decrease in the differences among them. The groups involved—the "ethnics" or the respective "bearers" of these cultures—would gradually disappear as organizational forms. This quite reasonable scholarly notion also carried ideological appeal. Karl Marx predicted the extinction of ethnic groups, asking, Why should one continue to belong to archaic cultural groupings when one could become a "worker"? And many American social scientists cherished the "liberal expectancy" that antagonisms would disappear by the mutual leveling of the cultures. Indeed, tribal communities in the Third World have been dismantled and much cultural diversity has been erased by modern institutions. The army, religious missions, public administration, urbanization, mass media, and schools all work in the same direction.

In the last 20 years, however, another trend has emerged on the world level, indicating that matters are somewhat more complex. To be sure, the process of acculturation will continue to cause many cultural differences to fade away. But new cultural differences will be introduced, sometimes in a deliberate manner. From the evidence presented in this book, I conclude that ethnic groups are affirming themselves more and more. They promote their own, new cultural identity, even as their old identity is eroded. This is a conclusion supported (even predicted) by the work of De Vos and Romanucci-Ross (1975), Glazer and Moynihan (1975), Thernstrom (1980), and others. In this book, I examine this prediction in the light of new, detailed case data, and find the results compelling. In addition, I also try—and I consider this to be my own contribution to theory—to develop renewed perspectives on the link between ethnic behavior on the one hand, and observable ideational and material development on the other.

RESEARCH AND CASE STUDIES

From 1974 to the present, I coordinated "The Culture of Ethnic Minorities" project at the Center of Social and Cultural Anthropology at Catholic University, Leuven. In that project, my research associates and I conducted long-term field studies among Sicilians in Sicily and Belgium (Leman, 1982), Berbers in Morocco and Belgium (Cammaert, 1985), Aymara Indians of the Altiplano of Bolivia (Pauwels, 1983), the Luba of Zaire (Mukendi, 1985), and the Huron Indians or Hurons of Quebec, Canada (Roosens, 1986).

In this book, I devote a considerable amount of attention to the Hurons and other Indians of Quebec because I followed them as a researcher from 1968 to 1982, and their particular case permits me to examine from a firsthand perspective how the formation and maintenance of ethnic identity and ethnicity proceeds in relation to that of other population groups. I will treat the Huron case in considerable detail, and I will trace comparisons in the other case studies published by members of our research team. Through these comparisons, I hope to identify similarities and differences in "how ethnicity works."

Each of the groups studied exists in a different historical context and has a different cultural tradition, but they are all variants of the same core phenomenon. The case of the Hurons shows how ethnicity can be constructed, almost from historical scratch; the Aymara demonstrate by their behavior that ethnicity does not result automatically from a strong, "objective" cultural continuity, but that the general, broad historical or political setting can play a decisive role. The case of the Luba of Kasai shows that a strong ethnic presentation, which has also been called retribalization by some authors when they are discussing developing countries, is not necessarily a return to an earlier, more "primitive" situation. The immigrants in Brussels illustrate how ethnicity can take various forms in a single city. That Brussels is the capital of a unifying Europe adds some flavor to the case.

I would like to stress that my work *is not* a reconstruction of the most recent developments among each of the peoples which our team studied. It rather is a reflection on a period stretching from 1968 to the early 1980s for most cases, and has to be considered in that light. An updating of further empirical developments in the various fields under study is beyond our means. Only the chapter on immigrant minorities in Belgium extends to 1989.

THEORETICAL STARTING POINT

The study of "tribalism" or "nationalism" is nothing new. One has to await the late 1960s and early 1970s, however, to witness a gradual development of sociological and anthropological theory on ethnic phenomena.

In this book I start from a synthesis of a few basic dimensions that have been brought to the foreground by a limited number of authors. These dimensions are: the ethnic group as a social vessel (Barth, 1969); ethnicity and the struggle for material goods and status (Glazer and Moynihan, 1975; Patterson, 1978); ethnic identification and social identification (Bell, 1975); and the sociopsychological dimensions of ethnicity (De Vos, 1975; Epstein, 1978). This theoretical framework provides a useful perspective to start the analysis of our materials.

Additional aspects of ethnicity can be found in the relationship between ethnic phenomena and observable, "objective" culture. This side of the question is somewhat neglected in recent theory. Since Barth, much attention has been given to the subjective side of ethnic belonging and to culture manipulation in interactive settings, thus detracting from culture as a source of causality sui generis.

Still another dimension deserves attention. There seems to be a far-reaching consensus among human beings, whatever their cultural tradition, that a number of material goods and social values, whose production originated in Western society, are highly desirable. As will be highlighted by the case studies, this quasi-universal consensus affects the cultural expression of ethnic formation and ethnic feelings in a direct way. I will focus closely on these two aspects throughout the different case studies and will develop a synthesis at the end of the book as a contribution to theory.

The Concept of "Ethnic Group"

Ethnic Groups and Observable Culture

The approach used by Barth in his book *Ethnic Groups and Boundaries* (1969) seems to me to be an appropriate point of departure for the clarification of concepts such as "ethnic group," "ethnic identity," "own culture." Barth states that a distinction should be made between, on the one hand, the ethnic organization of a group and the ethnic identification of individuals ("I am Flemish") and, on the other hand, the so-called objective, perceivable, investigatable culture by which the ethnic group was conceptually defined up until the late 1960s. In the former concept, the ethnic group was composed of people with a common culture and descent; the ethnic group consisted of the bearers of this culture. The terms "culture" and "ethnic group" were often used interchangeably. Barth pointed out that an ethnic group is, first of all, a form of social organization in which the participants themselves make use of certain cultural traits from their past, a past which may or may not be verifiable historically. It may well be that, in certain cases, the actors impute these cultural traits to themselves, as I will demonstrate in the chapters on the Hurons of Quebec. Cultural traits that are postulated as external emblems (clothing, language, etc.) or even as fundamental values (e.g., faithfulness in friendship) can thus be taken from one's own tradition or from other people's or simply may be created.

Self-Ascribed Culture and Social Boundaries

The cultural traits by which an ethnic group defines itself never comprise the totality of the observable culture but are only a combination of some characteristics that the actors ascribe to themselves and consider relevant. These traits can be replaced by others in the course of time. For the vindication of the ethnic group, it is sufficient that a social border be drawn between itself and similar groups by means of a few cultural emblems and values that make it different in its own eyes and in the eyes of others. Barth points out that the intensity with which a group profiles itself as an ethnic group, and with which individuals stress their ethnicity, generally increases when there is intense spatial–geographical and social contact between groups. The most isolated "traditional" group of people is probably the least ethnically self-defined. There is more chance that the Flemish in Brussels, who always have to speak French, will become more "consciously" Flemish than their ethnic brothers and sisters in the rather isolated rural areas of

West Flanders or Limburg. The "ethnic group" is thus not an organizational pattern that in its purest form would describe so-called primitive peoples from the earliest days of the colonial era. The study of LeVine and Campbell (1972) has convincingly shown that the isolated, culturally homogeneous tribe or ethnic unit was often the creation of the colonial administrator or the missionary who wanted to divide "his area" clearly into separate population groups, or of ethnographers or ethnologists who wanted to situate the "tribes" of a region conveniently on a map. Ethnic groups are generally the most clearly delineated in areas that have one or another form of overarching political organization.

Ethnicity and Economic Interest

Like several other authors who published after him or at the same time (1969), Barth points out that ethnic self-affirmation or the ignoring or minimalization of ethnic identity is always related in one or another way to the defense of social or economic interests. Many people change their ethnic identity only if they can profit by doing so.

Glazer and Moynihan, who have studied the ethnic groups of New York (1963) and North America (1975) extensively, subscribe to the same position. The recent emergence of ethnic groups in the United States is, in their opinion, largely though not exclusively due to how interests are promoted by the welfare state, for the U.S. government has become increasingly involved in economic matters since the 1960s. It subsidizes industry; manages the environment; acts to redistribute wealth to the less advantaged, the unemployed, the minorities, those discriminated against, and so forth. In such an atmosphere politicians acquire more and more power and, in a democratic system where leaders are selected by elections, pressure groups become ever more effective.

Now, the ethnic group in the United States is an appropriate instrument for applying pressure: those who are less advantaged (blacks, Hispanics, poor whites, Native Americans, and so on) may well belong to an ethnic category that as a whole feels less advantaged for historical reasons. Stressing this, the members of the group indirectly say that they are equal to every other group. Everybody is just as "different" from everybody else, and this is as it should be, the argument goes. Being just as good as anyone else becomes almost a kind of natural right, since nobody can help what his or her origin is. It becomes more interesting to appear socially as a member of an ethnic group than as a specimen of a lower socioeconomic

category. In a world where a reevaluation of "oppressed" cultures is in
vogue in many circles, this is a way of self-valorization that cannot be
achieved by considering oneself, for example, a member of the working
class or the lower middle class. If one identifies oneself as a member of
a lower class, one places oneself at the bottom of the social ladder. The
class division is vertical and is thus a hierarchical division of groups of
people; the ethnic division is horizontal, and it creates equivalencies rather
than hierarchies.

Ethnic Groups: Pressure Groups with a Noble Face

There were few advantages in the United States or Canada of the 1930s
to define oneself visibly as a member of the Sicilian or Polish immigrant
community. When one considers the current North American situation,
however, one concludes that ethnic groups emerged so strongly because
ethnicity brought people strategic advantages. Not so long ago it would have
been unthinkable for a court to order, as Judge Malouf did in Canada, the
stoppage of the gigantic, billion-dollar project of Hydro-Québec in northern
Quebec in 1975 because a few impecunious Indian leaders insisted on the
constitutional rights of their people (Gagnon, 1973). Ethnic groups allow
a positive self-image to be formed and at the same time meet what seems
to be an obvious need—the right to be culturally oneself and to receive the
means necessary to do so. Moreover, politicians can hardly say no to an
ethnic group without running the risk of being branded as racists. If they
refuse to favor the less economically advantaged or the members of a trade
union, they are, at best, "capitalists" or "conservatives." Militant ethnic
groups can thus be considered pressure groups with a noble face, at least
in the present North American context.

Glazer and Moynihan are not alone in their interpretation of ethnic groups
as pressure groups, and many other authors support this interpretation. This
model also seems to be a fruitful hypothesis for the understanding of interethnic relationships outside of North America. Patterson (1978) has applied
it to Chinese established in Jamaica and Guyana and has demonstrated that
the one group stresses and develops an ethnic profile because it is socioeconomically advantageous to do so, while the other group does not do it
at all for the same reason. Cohen (1969) gives an analogous interpretation
for the Hausa in Nigeria. LeVine and Campbell (1972) arrive at the same
conclusion on the basis of a comparative study of the anthropological
literature (up to 1972). More recently, in a book which is purposely limited

to severely divided societies in Asia, Africa, and the Caribbean, Horowitz (1985) tries to show that ethnicity is *not* necessarily concerned with socio-economic issues in every possible setting. I will not discuss Horowitz's position here because I have exclusively studied ethnic groups that do not stand in a hierarchical or ranked position to one another (Horowitz, 1985: 17). All other cases have been discarded. Horowitz is working in an interesting though quite different, field.

Some authors wonder how effective the ethnic–cultural rhetoric will actually be. Patterson (1978) believes that it will only yield superficial recognition on the part of the dominant groups in the United States, while the socioeconomic power relationships will remain largely unchanged. The dominant ethnic groups will play the game without being taken in by it: statements will be issued, it will be said that the specific culture and cultural values of the less-advantaged ethnic groups are "recognized" and, if need be, some insignificant sums will be invested. Nevertheless, there will be an attempt to maintain the real foundation of the power relationship unimpaired, the socioeconomic structure. Hannerz (1976) reasons in the same way. Several Indian leaders whom I met in the course of my research on the Hurons of Quebec fear an analogous development, even though they have never before been enveloped in so much "recognition" and ceremony by the Canadian authorities.

Ethnic Identity: A Psychological Reality

The mobilization of ethnic groups is only possible because political leaders are able to rely on profound affective factors related to origin, such as sharing "the same blood" and being faithful to a tradition handed down from one generation to the other. De Vos (1975), Epstein (1978), and others have devoted particular attention to this noneconomic, psychosocial dimension of ethnic identity. Together with these authors, I believe that the individual must be seen in his or her social dimensions if we are to understand both the success and the driving force of individual and collective ethnic self-affirmation. The concept of "identity" is traced by De Vos and Epstein to social psychology in the sense that an "internal," intrapsychic dimension can be identified in it, in addition to a social dimension referring to "the others."

Both dimensions are closely interwoven. Every person experiences the sense of belonging to one or another social category, network, or group and knows that he or she is partially determined by it: one is like others who also belong to the same unit and different from others who are members of comparable units. Each individual always belongs to several social units: a nation, a profession, a family, a political party, an ethnic group, a religious organization, and so on, and belongs to all of them at the same time. One is aware of belonging to these groups, networks, and categories, and is so recognized and identified by others, members and nonmembers, in terms of this belonging. Generally, the individual prefers one or the other identity, so that there is a hierarchy of identities for each person: one is first of all a Belgian, then a Fleming, a train conductor, a Catholic, and so forth. This hierarchy can be inverted or changed in time, or one social identity can simply be more relevant than others in a given context: in a Flemish demonstration in Brussels, it makes little difference if I am a pilot, a veterinarian, or a baker.

It is possible that an ethnic identity will be assigned a comprehensive role in certain circumstances. In South Africa, for example, ethnic identity determines a series of identities in the social, political, cultural, and economic sectors. Because of one's ethnic identity, one is enclosed in some realities and simultaneously excluded from others. But ethnic identity may have no significance. In certain types of society, individuals may, for their entire lives or for very long periods, assign only limited value to, or may ignore altogether, what would theoretically be their ethnic allegiance, and their social environment can support them in this. Not all geographical Flemings are "conscious" Flemings. Even in a country such as Belgium, with its strong political conflicts between the "communities," there are thousands of people who never affirm themselves ethnically, and one even encounters those who refuse to do so on principle because they see the struggle between Flemings and Walloons as a petty fuss. Given our current knowledge, nobody could maintain that ethnic identity is a "feeling" that is determined by genes or by "the blood," and that one carries it with oneself in all circumstances of life.

Those who do identify with an ethnic category, network, or group can find psychological security in this identification, a feeling of belonging, a certainty that one knows one's origin, that one can live on in the younger generations of one's people who will carry on the struggle, and so on. One can commit oneself to "a cause," fulfill oneself, realize oneself to be unique, original, irreplaceable as a member of an ethnic group and irreducible from the outside to something else. After all, nobody can change "the past" from which one descends, and nobody can undo who one is. One can feel oneself to be different from the others, and in this being different define and experience oneself as incomparable or as *primordially* equal.

What the precise "historical and cultural realities" or historical data are that are taken as starting points have no importance for the individual from a psychological perspective. The ethnic "past" is always a subjective reconstruction. It is quite possible to feel myself a full-blooded Fleming even though most of my ancestors were Spaniards who remained in Belgium after the Spanish period if I do not know it or if it was long enough ago so that no one realizes it or considers it relevant. Some of these psychological effects can also be obtained by stressing membership in a religion. Ethnicity need not be involved. But the fact is that many people do identify themselves in terms of ethnic identity.

The 1960s and 1970s: A Propitious Time for Ethnicity

In fact, this does not seem to be a matter of chance according to Bell (1975), a sociologist and political scientist. After an analysis of the current cultural cycle in the industrialized countries of the West, Bell postulates that more people identify themselves ethnically than in years past because the ethnic unit is one of the few organizational forms that, on the macro-level, offers stability in a time of decline of authority in all its forms. The class struggle has become a verbal battle around a negotiation table.

The nation, too, has lost much of its ideological foundation and power of attraction because there are only a few countries left which emphasize a truly national ideology and because there have been no wars between the nations of the West since World War II. The communal enemy has become a bloc of states, not any single nation. In addition, entities such as the United Nations have not yet developed an ideology ("lay spirituality") that can appeal to many people.

The Flexibility of Ethnic Identification

An ethnic category, network, or group, however, offers, from the social point of view, communality in language, a series of customs and symbols, a style, rituals, an appearance, and so forth, which can penetrate life in many ways. These trappings of ethnicity are particularly attractive when one is continually confronted by others who live differently, as happens in New York, Paris, Brussels, and Amsterdam. If I see and experience myself as a member of an ethnic category or group, and others—fellow members and outsiders—recognize me as such, "ways of being" become possible for me that set me apart from the outsiders. These ways of being contribute to the *content* of my self-perception. In this sense, I *become* my ethnic allegiance; I experience any attack on the symbols, emblems, or values (cultural elements) that define my ethnicity as an attack on myself. The "right to one's own culture" and "the right to preserve one's own ethnic identity" are usually presented as inalienable and as pertaining to the sphere of "human rights."

Ethnic identification can go on rather militantly within an explicitly organized group, as was the case with the Black Panthers in the United States during the 1960s. But it can also affect the lives of individuals: how they dress, the language they speak when they go shopping or when they discipline their children, how (or even whether) they interact with government agencies, and the newspaper(s) they read. It can affect the choice of a spouse, the formation of a circle of friends, how children are raised, and how one behaves emotionally (that is, effusively or with reserve). Virtually anything that has not already been explicitly or publicly affirmed by members of other ethnic groups as ethnic emblems can, in principle, become an emblem of ethnicity for other groups. *Visible* distinctions between socio-economic levels have become vaguer in modern industrialized societies than they were in the past; it is more difficult now to identify oneself as a member of a professional category or of a "social class" simply by virtue of dress or cosmetic emblems. In an intense, multiethnic milieu, however, one can make use of any number of signs for differentiation as long as they are credible—that is, so long as they *could* be in line with a particular cultural tradition.

Political Manipulation

It is obvious that ethnic self-esteem is susceptible to all kinds of political manipulation. The less critical can be led to believe that the "ethnic feeling" is a primordial, essential dimension of every human being, that it is inborn in the blood, that one can almost feel it physically, that one must fight to safeguard this "high value," that one is indebted to the ancestors from whom one has received life and "everything." Political leaders can create stereotypes that give almost religious exaltedness to ethnic identity and, via stereotypes, lead to economic and cultural wars with other groups and even to genocide. It is also possible to sing the praises of the "multiethnic community of tolerance," to point to the "richness" of the "cultural mosaic" within a city or a state, and most national leaders of multiethnic countries do so regularly.

The Many Faces of Ethnicity

The term "ethnic identity" can thus stand for an entire range of phenomena, going from what Gans (1979) calls symbolic ethnicity, that is, ethnicity that manifests itself superficially and temporarily, to the comprehensive commitment of the ethnic leader figure who professionally organizes the interethnic struggle.

In the elasticity of the expression "ethnic identity," the dynamic character of the cultural, the social, and the psychological becomes visible in combination; these three dimensions overlap each other and make many nuances possible. The term "ethnic identity" can, for example, refer to origin, uniqueness, passing on of life, "blood," solidarity, unity, security, personal integrity, independence, recognition, equality, cultural uniqueness, respect, equal economic rights, territorial integrity, and so on, and these in all possible combinations, degrees of emotional content, and forms of social organization. It is, therefore, not at all surprising that the words "ethnic group," "culture," and "ethnic identity" are confused in daily usage: ethnicity can only be manifested by means of cultural forms that give the impression that they are inherent to a particular category or group of individuals. It is impossible for ethnic identity to mean anything without the existence of ethnic groups or categories, for it is a relational construct.

In the following chapters, I will analyze different aspects of ethnicity treated in the preceding section, starting with the Indian question in Quebec as it developed between 1968 and 1982. I will first discuss Indians in Canada in general, and then focus specifically on the Huron Indians of Quebec.

Chapter 2, on Indian status, dramatically illustrates the making of ethnic groups as molded by the white majority leaders of Canada and as imposed on the Amerindian groups of Canada. The way Indian status is defined shows constructive activity at work, almost in a pure form. Logic is applied in delimiting ethnic status, but in such a way that the maximization of white predominance in all fields of the life of the society is fully guaranteed. Only the "biological fact" that a child of two "pure Indian" parents is itself a "pure Indian" is taken as an undeniable given. Ethnic status accorded non-Indians who marry Indians and the children born from such marriages is construed so that the reproduction of registered Indians is kept at a minimum. For instance, the children of a registered Indian man and an Egyptian woman are registered Indians, but the children of his registered Indian sister and a non-Indian, become non-Indians. At the time these regulations were devised, many more white men married Indian women than Indians married white women. No choice of ethnic membership was left to individual persons in this matter, nor was agreement sought with the groups of Indians who were affiliated through such mixed marriages.

The historical development of the definition of ethnicity by the Indian law shows how ethnic definitions changed or at least were contested by the Indians when power relations between Canadians and Indian autochthons shifted as a result of the postcolonial international climate. Both expressive and instrumental factors can be seen at work: meaning and practical reason.

The case of the Hurons, on the other hand, displays ethnic creation operating on the Amerindian side. Within 20 years, not only was a self-conscious people created, starting from very few cultural relics of an Indian past, but this resurrected ethnic group also became fully accepted as a nation by Canadian leaders, at least in the public forum.

I would point out again that this case study is not meant to demonstrate in a cynical way how naive Canadians were forced by Indian arm twisting and deception to recognize a nonexistent Indian people as a reality to be dealt with. It merely shows what happens when human beings construct what they call "reality," a process that is going on all over the world in every sector of culture.

What follows makes clear that different readings of the same phenomena do coexist: Grand Chief Gros-Louis, in his book on his people and on the Indian question in general, provides a different picture from that of a number of distinguished historians and of the committee of experts who expressed their view in the "Rapport Dorion," while the Parti Québecois—itself a nationalistic movement—almost totally ignores the existence of Indian peoples on the "French Canadian" soil. The alarming socioeconomic situation and poor health of many Amerindian groups, as described in *Les Indiens*, are ignored by the various parties for different reasons.

The most credible view of what is really at the heart of Amerindian ethnic groups in the 1960s and 1970s emerges from discussions with the members of the Huron community. These residents of the Huron Village, though very much concerned about their future, illuminate certain portions of reality and conceal others.

In all these versions, however, reference to the "truth" is never far away. Even the most daring misrepresentation claims to be the truth, to be something "out there," a piece of reality independent of what people say. Nobody accepts pure relativism.

-2-

INDIAN STATUS

THE INDIANS, CANADA, AND QUEBEC

From 1968–1982, the time of this study, Canada was caught up in an anachronistic situation: it was still colonizing its own national territory. Sometimes called the Switzerland of the New World, Canada has had to cope for the last 20 years with increasing resistance by indigenous populations against this colonization. The Indians and the Inuit claim that they still have rights, however vague those may be according to Western legal norms, over gigantic amounts of territory. From the Canadian national perspective, these rights have yet to be "extinguished."

For example, in 1912, the Province of Quebec accepted the obligation, stipulated in the Royal Proclamation of 1763, to buy out the rights of Indian and Inuit people over parcels of territory that up until then had been under the control of the federal government. To this day, vast areas of land have never been militarily conquered or even inhabited by the French, English or, later, Canadians. Nor has that land been formally relinquished by the native peoples. This allows the Indians and Inuit to say that, under norms of Western law, the appropriation of the land of their forefathers is largely a legal fiction, a one-sided declaration put on paper by the colonizers without the agreement of the owners.

This position is not a product of some exaggerated Indian ideology or of Canadian environmentalists. It is based on a growing body of legal precedent. In 1975, the James Bay Convention was signed, on the one hand, by groups of Cree Indians and Inuit and, on the other, by the federal government, the Province of Quebec, and private companies. The convention was ratified in 1978, with the result that the Cree and Inuit surrendered 250,000 square miles of land but retained exclusive or special rights to still larger areas of their ancestral land. The 12,000 native people involved were awarded collective compensation of 225 million Canadian dollars, to be paid over a period of 20 years. Thus, for about 1,000 dollars per native per year for 20 years, the private companies and the government received the right to build hydroelectric power stations in the area.

Among Indian and Inuit leaders who were not involved in the negotiations, the James Bay Convention has been branded as the latest colonial scandal. This position is also reflected in many national-level publications. The agreement is seen in these circles as immoral—the most recent treaty in a series whereby autochthons are pressured by the state and the multinationals to sign agreements that lead to the disappearance of native people and that annul rights rather than compensate for their loss. Actually, the rate of compensation has been considerably improved compared to earlier treaties by which enormous territories were ceded for a few dollars per person per year and the annual delivery by the government of small amounts of gunpowder, rope, new clothes for the leaders of the group, and similar trifles. But the James Bay affair nonetheless continued this tradition of exploitation more than 20 years after the decolonization of Africa.

Both the federal and the provincial authorities were disturbed by the problem as it could damage the image of Canada internationally. But more than image was at stake. As a Western, industrialized nation, Canada is involved in stiff international economic competition. The national unemployment rate was more than 12% in the fall of 1982 (in the United States it was then 10%); it was more than 13% in the Province of Quebec and still higher in Newfoundland. Rapid exploitation of all natural resources seems to be imperative, and vast, untapped resources are situated precisely in the northern territories that the autochthons continue to claim.

One might think that, with only about 320,000 autochthons in Canada and at most 28,000 in Quebec, the issue would be rapidly resolved. But, in fact, this small minority was acting with increasing success in turning four centuries of colonization against 25 million Canadians. The gradual dismantling and assimilation of indigenous groups was significantly retarded in the 1960s.

For the federal and provincial authorities of Canada, the resistance of the autochthons was unexpected. The contents of a political proposal, known as the "white paper of 1969" and published by the Ministry for Indian Affairs, shows that the authorities were not accurately informed about the lives and feelings of native peoples. Minister J. Chrétien produced what he thought was a lure for the Indians and the Inuit, but the proposal turned out to be precisely what they did not want and never had wanted, namely, to disappear as a special category of the population. In his text, the minister admitted that the Indians and the Inuit were treated unjustly in the past, that they had not been given equal opportunities, that the bureaucratic apparatus, which functioned as their guardian and administered them in almost all areas of life, was not capable of providing them with what they had a right to, and that this agency would thus be abolished within five years, along with the obsolete reservation system and the Indian Act, which granted special status to native peoples. All forms of discrimination would be eliminated, and the autochthons would become full-fledged citizens. All of this would take place with full respect for the native culture, in the context of a "just society" that would be structured multiculturally, according to the minister. Extra economic support would be granted to the autochthons because of their less favorable socioeconomic position. This white paper caused a massive reaction from Indians and Inuit throughout Canada. The response was a categorical "no," and the Canadian government was eventually forced by the evolution of events to drop this proposal completely.

Since then, political activity among Indians has moved increasingly into the public forum, and a dialectic has developed between ethnic groups, governments, and local leaders over international ethics and socioeconomics. In the major case study presented here, I will analyze these relations as they developed between 1968 and 1982, from the perspective of the Huron Indians of Quebec. The Hurons are a people who have sought to recapture their ethnicity, after being nearly obliterated culturally.

WHO IS AN INDIAN?
"NATURE" AND ETHNIC ENGINEERING

People in Canada speak easily about "the Indians," "the autochthons" (Amerindians and Inuit or Eskimos), and nobody seems to have any difficulty with these terms. There are "Indian reservations," and there are "Indian crafts." More than 30 magazines are published by Indians, and the Ministry of Indian Affairs and Northern Development (MIAND) regularly publishes reports, texts, and brochures related to the Indians. Indians are a recognized reality in the national community. And yet, who is recognized or should be recognized as an Indian is still under negotiation. In 1984, the question had been under discussion for more than 10 years between the federal government and a number of Indian leaders with, apparently, no agreement being reached. Ethnic boundaries have not been precisely delineated, and the problem is not that "whites" refuse to accept Indians into their dominant community. On the contrary, the pressure is on Indians to assimilate, to blend into the white community. Despite this, tens of thousands of people in Canada are demanding Indian status. They generally belong to associations of *métis* or *Indians without status*, and these organizations are found everywhere in Canada. Many more people in Canada want to be Indians than the government has hitherto permitted.

One might imagine that Indians would simply be those who are biologically unmixed. But this is far from the case. Considered phenotypically and biologically, the officially recognized Indians and the métis and the nonstatus Indians are overlapping populations. Among the nonstatus Indians and also among those who call themselves métis, many are biologically as close to the precontact autochthons of 500 years ago as many Indians recognized by law. The degree of phenotypical overlap between these social categories varies from region to region and cannot be determined with precision. On highly isolated reservations, there has been very little mixing with non-Indians. In the South, however, near cities like Quebec and Montreal, a lot of exogamy has taken place. In the last decade, one Indian out of two married a non-Indian partner (*Elimination*, 1982: 4). This trend is particularly strong in the urbanized reservations.

Who, then, are the métis and who the Indians? According to the Indian Act of 1951 (pp. 4–10), an Indian is someone who is officially registered as an Indian by the registrar, the high government official who maintains the Indian register. Thus, non-Indians determine who is officially an Indian and who is not. The 1951 version of the Indian Act is the final product of a long series of legal reforms that established, among other things, the criteria one had to satisfy in order to be registered as an Indian. This law unmistakably assumes that the ethnic qualification of "Indian" is principally related to and based on biological *generation* or filiation: a child of two "full-blood" Indians is, without any doubt, an Indian, but one who deviates too much from this ideal type is not. The law thus states, at least implicitly, that ethnic belonging is concerned with biological descent. But the law is culturebound as far as borderline cases are concerned. Since 1951, to be registered as an Indian one has to be the legitimate child of an Indian father. The ethnic origin of the mother is irrelevant: she could be French, English, Egyptian, Turkish, or whatever. Furthermore, if the grandmother on the Indian side of a mixed marriage (the father's mother) is a non-Indian by descent, then the grandchild loses his or her status at the age of 21. Thus, one can be officially born an Indian and lose this status at the age of maturity. By contrast, no problems arise at all for a non-Indian mother married to an Indian father of a child: any woman who marries a registered Indian becomes ipso facto an Indian, and so are her children.

The same law separates still more spectacularly the biological from the sociocultural: if an Indian woman marries a non-Indian, she loses her Indian status. The children of her marriage cannot be registered as Indians.

According to the Indian Act, then, "Indian blood" can only be transmitted by the father. Children of Indian fathers are Indians; children of white fathers are whites. The law regarding illegitimate children is somewhat more complicated (Indian Act, p. 7), and I will return to this later. Let us first look more closely at the legal mechanism with which racial–ethnic groups are produced and reproduced in Canada and examine the effects these modalities have on the lives of individuals and groups.

THE HISTORICAL DEVELOPMENT OF INDIAN STATUS: ETHNIC DEFINITIONS AS A TOOL OF EXTINCTION

As might be expected, Indians are considered to be like minor children who need protection, so others must decide who can be included among them and who not. The 1951 law, like its predecessors, was passed by the Canadian parliament in consultation with the Department for Indian Affairs with little participation by Indians.

That law cannot be understood without examining the global relations between colonizers and colonized, allochtons and autochthons, as these relations developed in the course of history. Numerous publications (e.g., Trigger, 1976; Martin, 1978) show that many Indians—and this applies particularly to the Indians of Quebec—were indispensable trading partners for the French and the English up to the first decades of the nineteenth century. The fur trade was very important to the European colonizers of that era, and this profitable activity could not have been maintained without the active cooperation of the Indian hunters and trappers, including Montagnais, Algonquins, Naskapi, and others. Most Indian groups were self-supporting, and the sums invested by the French in the Montagnais, Huron, and other reservations were ridiculously small in comparison with the profits derived from the fur trade (Trigger, 1976: 803). From the colonizers' perspective, the Indians and their hunting and trapping skills had to be preserved. Hunting and setting traps were activities that required a thorough knowledge of the environment and the mastery of complex techniques. The French and the English were incompetent in these areas, and very few Euro-Canadians were prepared to take on the severe apprenticeship required to become hunters and trappers.

Nevertheless, the idea that the Indians had to continue to produce game for the French was not irreconcilable in the initial colonial period with the idea that Indians should assimilate, both biologically and culturally. The

French authorities considered it advisable for white men to marry autochthon women. These marriages were, first of all, practical: there was a shortage of women of European origin, and the Indian women, better than their European sisters, knew all sorts of nutritional and cooking techniques that permitted survival over the severe winters. In addition, the mixed, interracial marriages had a "civilizing" effect on the "savages." And it was also a technique for religious conversion. Officially, at least, the English colonizers adopted a different ideology and segregated Indians onto reserves. But this did not prevent frequent deviations from the ideology in practice (Jamieson, 1978: 15–16).

The large number of marriages with Indian women did not threaten Indian hunting production, since this was in the hands of the men. Nor was there a danger that future generations of Indians would be absorbed by the French colony via mixed marriages. The number of mixed marriages was not that large, and often the children from them were simply integrated into the group of the mother. In other words, during colonial times it was of little importance to both the Indians and the whites how the ethnicity of borderline cases was determined.

Still, from the beginning, the French initiated these marriages, while the Indians did not approve of them (Jamieson, 1978: 15–16). The métis of Canada, in other words, came into existence (as métis did in many other countries of the world) at the initiative of the colonizer. This point is not unimportant for the evaluation of the way in which Parliament would later treat the métis.

Marriages between Europeans and Indians were generally not church weddings but common-law contracts that were maintained for years and sometimes for life, but which could also be broken by the return of the white husband to his country of origin or on the occasion of his Catholic marriage to a white woman. Not all the white authorities supported this assimilation policy. Trigger (1976: 367–369, 718–719) clearly shows that the missionaries of the Society of Jesus, who conducted an apostolate among the Indians of Quebec in the seventeenth century, rejected the assimilation bonds. The Jesuits argued, on the basis of their missionary method, that the sexual activity of French adventurers could do considerable harm.

However that may be, the mixing took place and also continued in later times. Although nobody can calculate this precisely, some specialists (*Rapport de la Commission*, 1971: 89) believe that one Canadian out of four has Indian ancestors. The cases of registered Indians who have whites among their ancestors are legion. This applies particularly to the more urbanized reservations of Quebec, such as the Huron Village and Kahnawake (or Caughnawaga).

The Indians, as separate ethnic groups, became a definitive hindrance for the Canadians when the full expansion to the West began in the course of the nineteenth century. The objective of the colonists at the time was to occupy the Western territories as quickly as possible and thus establish claim to them before the United States, which had become independent, could do so. When the authorities recruited ever more immigrants from Europe with the promise that each family could receive a piece of free land, the removal of the autochthon owners became urgent. A whole series of treaties was concluded with the Indians whereby the autochthon proprietors, generally under great pressure, were led to yield their extended territories to the Crown for small sums of money, some material goods, and the setting apart of reservations. The goods listed in the treaties—for example, a suit of clothes every three years for the chief, rope, gunpowder, beads, and sums of four or five dollars per head—have since become symbols of the exploitation to which the autochthons were subjected during colonial times. But even these minimal obligations that had been entered into in exchange for gigantic territories (Savard and Proulx, 1982: 114) appeared to some politicians as burdensome: they were expenses borne by the "hard-working" whites for the accommodation of the Indian "loafers" (Savard and Proulx, 1982: 80 ff.), expenditures that had to be limited as much as possible. It was, therefore, considered advisable to restrict and reduce the number of Indians to whom were due the per capita payments or whose reservation lands one wanted to acquire.

Jamieson (1978), to whose work I regularly refer in these pages, has clearly demonstrated how the legislation became ever more restrictive. In the years 1860 and 1870, members of Parliament and other authorities specifically gave consideration to ways of reducing the number of Indians who were wards of the state. In 1850, Indian status was allotted rather generously: whoever was descended from Indians, paternally or maternally, and whoever was married to an Indian, or had lived with a group of Indians for a considerable period of time, could have himself or herself registered as an Indian. The text reads as follows:

> First, all Indians of pure blood, known to belong to the tribe or particular clan of Indians interested in the said land and their descendants. Second, all persons married to Indians and residing among them and the descendants of such persons. Third, all persons residing among the Indians of which the parents on both

sides were or are Indians of such a tribe or clan or have the right of being considered as such. Fourth, all persons adopted in their infancy by Indians and
residing in the village or on the land of the Indian tribe or clan, and their descendants. (*Historique de la loi sur les Indiens*, 1980: 32)

Very soon, however, limitations began to be imposed: in the legal
prescriptions of 1869, the granting of membership in an Indian group was
determined exclusively patrilineally. Jamieson points out that over time a
large number of Indian groups have protested against the loss of Indian status
by their women and that they could no longer live on the reservation if they
married a non-Indian. These protests, however, have had no effect on the
law.

For the authorities of the nineteenth century—and this seems to have been
a universal colonial phenomenon—it was obvious that their interventions
objectively benefited the Indians. Indeed, it was thought that granting the
children of a Euro-Canadian father who was married to an Indian the status
of their father was a social promotion: these children could thus have access to the French or English culture, two civilizations that towered over
the life customs of the Indians, who did not even have a "true culture."
In the nineteenth century, it was certain for many scholars that the patrilineal
form of transmission was a more highly evolved cultural pattern than the
matrilineal (*Historique*, 1980: 193–194).

It is in this perspective of the cultural superiority of the whites that one
must place the institution that permitted the "evolved" Indians to request
emancipation. An Indian who considered that he had acquired enough
"civilization" could, during a trial period, prove that he was capable of
supporting himself in the society without any form of help or protection.
In this way, he could be "emancipated" from his Indian status. The Law
of June 10, 1857 states the following in this regard:

> If these commissioners report by writing to the governor that an Indian, not under
> twenty-one years of age, can speak, read, and write either the English language
> or the French language fluently and well, and that he is sufficiently advanced
> in the elementary branches of education, and that he has a good moral character,
> and that he is not in debt—then the governor can have it announced in the Of-
> ficial Gazette of this province that this Indian is emancipated by virtue of the
> present act. (*Historique*, 1980: 37)

This emancipation procedure recalls analogous institutions that functioned
on other continents during the colonial period. For example, there was the

carte d'évolué that was issued in the former Belgian Congo to Africans who had demonstrated that they could live in the European manner.

Voluntary emancipation after application was not the only emancipation formula. If an Indian was emancipated, his wife and minor children were also emancipated, without their having requested it. Only after 1951 was this rule suspended and the consent of the wife was required before proceeding to emancipation (*Elimination*, 1982: 17). Other forms of emancipation were also conceived: the Indian who became a doctor of medicine, jurist, priest, or missionary was transferred to the status of ordinary citizen with full rights and lost his Indian status and its associated rights and duties. This measure illustrates official thinking about the various ethnic groups: anyone who had been promoted *culturally* and socioeconomically was also ethnically "elevated," his phenotypical characteristics and his ancestry aside. During one period of this century (Jamieson, 1978: 44, 52), the authorities could decide who was to be emancipated without the agreement of the person involved. This decision formula was only applied for a short period because of numerous protests against its use. From the historical sources it is clear that behind the policies of emancipation was a policy to decrease the number of Indians as quickly as possible.

Voluntary emancipation, however, does not seem to have been a success. At one time, there circulated in Parliament the ironic observation that it would take 36,000 years before all the Indians of Canada would be emancipated at the current rate (Jamieson, 1978: 47).

Initially, someone could inherit Indianness from both the father's and the mother's side but, by 1869, the law coupled ethnic belonging to the male line. After all, many white men commonly married Indian women, but few Indian men married white women. By forcing children to acquire the status of their father, the growth of the Indian population was efficiently limited. Moreover, if people were allowed to claim ethnicity from their mothers, or from either their fathers or their mothers, white men would have been allowed to reside on the reservations while preserving their Euro-Canadian status (which was contrary to other stipulations of the law) or they would have been forced to become "Indian." This last measure would have artificially increased the number of Indians. In addition, according to the prevailing European ideas of relations between men and women, it probably seemed more "fitting" that the wife would "follow" her husband than the reverse, and it certainly must have seemed fairer for children to share in the status of their white fathers than in that of their Indian mother. Indeed, it would hardly have been conceivable in the early nineteenth century for a white man, against his will, to be given the Indian status of his wife.

The laws regarding Indians were formulated, promulgated, and applied without serious consultation with the Indians. By imposing these laws of identity on all Indians, the Canadian government determined who would be considered a member of Canadian society and who would not. By the application of the Indian law, white women who married Indians became Indians and Indian women who married whites were transformed into French and English persons. The child of the brother became an Indian and the child of his sister a "white."

Some authors have stressed the "genocidal" aspect of the Indian law (Hargous, 1980: 12–44). In all fairness, the Canadian government in the nineteenth century could just as well have stated that an Indian was a person who had at least three grandparents of Indian origin and could have declared those who did not satisfy this criterion to be métis. Moreover, it was not until 1951 that both grandparents on the side of the Indian father had to be of Indian origin for someone to be "Indian." Among those recognized as Indians in 1951, many may have had much less than "50% Indian blood" in their veins. Furthermore, the government could have refused to grant Indian status to white women who married Indians, and this would have limited the Indian population still more. But the legislatures of the nineteenth century never promulgated these more stringent rules, perhaps because many bands were composed of "mixed" populations already during the time of the first law. This was certainly the case for the groups that lived near the larger cities.

THE ETHNIC "MUTATION" OF WOMEN:
AN UNFAIR DEAL

The patrilineal structure imposed by the 1951 law had considerable effects on individuals. If a woman was removed from the Indian register after her marriage, she had to leave the reservation territory. In some cases, young married couples were allowed to settle on the reservation as "Canadian" outsiders in rented accommodations. Among the Hurons of Lorette, for example, there were hundreds of tenants on the reservation in 1968 when I did fieldwork there. The band itself rented to outsiders houses that were the community property of the group. In cases where a reservation is near a city or a village, a married daughter can live off the reservation and still be in the immediate vicinity of her relatives. But these solutions are in-applicable on reservations with a housing shortage or those far from urban centers. A woman's possessions are to be sold to the highest bidder, and she is removed from the Indian register. She cannot inherit a house located on the reservation, even if the house belonged to her parents and even if she is the only legatee. The official rupture with her ethnic group also means segregation from her immediate family, whether she wishes it or not.

Like the emancipated Indians, Indian women who are removed from the register receive their share of the reservation-based capital and of the yields of the capital. This is paid out in a fixed sum, representing what she would otherwise have received, over a period of 20 years. But the sum is usually a pittance. Jamieson gives several examples: in May 1975, the Attawapiskat paid 7 cents and an annuity of $80; the Abegweit of Prince Edward Island awarded $4.06 in December 1975; the Montagnais of Escoumains, $4.45 in 1965. It is true that some rich bands in the West (which have shares in oil and gas operations on their reservations) pay out sums up to $12,000. Even in these cases, those marrying out are generally disadvantaged because not all the possessions and income of the band are considered when shares are calculated. The parties themselves have no right to examine the accounts and the files that give the exact size of the possessions and the income of the band (Jamieson, 1978: 68).

In recent years, now that all sorts of special social and cultural advan-tages are being granted to the autochthons, being dropped from the register means a considerable loss for a woman and her future family. Indians who live on a reservation pay no taxes on the income earned on the territory of the reservation. Nor do they pay provincial taxes on goods bought on the reservation, and in some provinces like Quebec no indirect taxes are collected on goods that are purchased off the reservation but delivered on it. Moreover, the children of exogamous women cannot benefit from the bicultural education provided on some reservations, nor do they receive free school lunches, books, trips, athletic equipment, maintenance grants, and so on. The special benefits that the government provides to autochthons who want to go on to higher education, such as free registration, free books, housing, and travel, are lost to the former Indian woman herself and her children (Jamieson, 1978: 70).

Many people who have been affected by this law feel that they have been treated unjustly. In mid-1982 there were 15,744 women in Canada who had lost their Indian status by the voluntary emancipation of their husbands. More than 40,000 children, without their having any opportunity to choose, have never received Indian rights because their mothers were married to

a non-Indian. There were also still 1,120 people alive who had been involuntarily emancipated (*Elimination*, 1982: 19-20). Other categories of
people also felt they had been deprived of their rights—people such as
children of Indians who were born after the emancipation of their parents.
The number of these people cannot be estimated. Then there are the descendants of Indians who, because of one or another administrative happen-
stance or because of the neglect of their parents, were never registered as
Indians but who still identify themselves as Indians.

The government has thus declared tens of thousands of people to be
"whites" who are biologically as related to the pre-Columbian autochthons
as their counterparts who live on a reservation. Legally, the matter seems
to be in order, but socially and politically the assimilation law has failed.
In the Province of Quebec alone, as many people are demanding Indian
status as there are legally registered Indians—approximately 25,000
(Gauvreau, Bernèche, and Fernandez, 1982: 95-104).

"NATURE" BOUNCES BACK

Although there have been protests in the last 110 years against the way
in which Indian status has been described, mass reactions have only come
in the last 20 years. Carried along by the world movement for equal rights
for women and because of the pressure exercised by the Canadian women's
movement in particular, the Canadian federal government in 1967 invited
the submission of complaints on the matter of the unequal administration
of justice between men and women. Among the women who sent in complaints were former Indian women who had lost their status by marriage
to a non-Indian. The question of the discrimination that is encompassed
in the Indian law rapidly became urgent because of the cause célèbre of
Jeannette Lavell, who tried to recover her lost status through the courts.
Lavell lost in the lower court, won on appeal, and lost again before the
Supreme Court, though by only one vote. This case clearly revealed the
staggering complexity of an apparently simple matter: in addition to the
Ministry for Indian Affairs and the Ministry of Justice, very influential Indian organizations opposed Lavell. At one level, Lavell was fighting against
her own people (Jamieson, 1978: 79-88).

When the White Paper of Minister J. Chrétien was published in 1969,
the reaction of Indian leaders over all of Canada was overwhelmingly
negative. The minister of Indian Affairs and Northern Development pro-

posed dismantling the special status for the Indians, guaranteed by law, within a period of five years (*La politique indienne du Gouvernement du Canada*, 1969: 9, 14). Influential Indian leaders demanded the maintenance of the special status until an agreement could be reached between the government and the Indian leaders over changes in the law. Indian leaders opposed Lavell because if she had won in court, it could have set a dangerous precedent: it could have implied that the laws applied to the general Canadian population would take precedence over the Indian Act, and the government would have a means of dismantling the Indian status indirectly. Of course, Parliament could do this at any time. The White Paper of 1969 left no doubt about this. But by then, outright abolition of the law, without the consent of the Indians, was not feasible. An indirect approach to getting around the special status law, however, was a real threat. The position that Indian leaders adopted by opposing Lavell was understandable in this context and need not necessarily have been motivated by antifeminism, as Jamieson (1978: 79–88) and others have suggested.

But there is still much more. Equalizing the rights of men and women would have given tens of thousands—some say hundreds of thousands—of individuals the right to return to the reservations. An Indian wife could make her white Canadian husband a full-fledged Indian by her marriage. Equalization might imply that he could live on a reservation with as much right as any descendant of Indians to participate in the governance of the reservation, to be exempt from taxation, and to benefit from the income intended as compensation for the rights that earlier generations of Indians yielded to the Crown. The millions of dollars that come annually to "oil reservations" would have to be divided among many more people. Not only the non-Indian husband, but also his children and descendants could continue to benefit from their Indian rights if they so wished. Giving Indian women precisely the same rights as Indian men would have had major material consequences. Furthermore, infiltration by strangers onto the reservation would have doubled. Just as many Indian men now marry non-Indian women as Indian women marry non-Indian men. Non-Indian, "alien" men are perceived differently in reservation communities than are women who marry into them. The fear is that the men are more apt to make use of their political rights than are women.

The addition of a large number of outsiders to the population of the reservations would give the government a dangerous argument: after a time, it could argue that the population of the reservations was no longer "authentically" Indian and that there would thus no longer be any sense in granting the reservations and their residents any special status. Particularly on the reservations situated near urban centers (where the number of "mixed" marriages is constantly increasing) one could expect absorption if the non-Indians and their "mixed" descendants were added to the bands.

In the meantime, the Canadian government decided to do nothing before the Indians themselves had formulated proposals. As far as I was able to observe in September and October of 1982, no solutions were to be expected in the near future.

THE LOGICAL MUDDLES OF ETHNIC ENGINEERING

"To facilitate the discussion," the Minister of Indian Affairs and Northern Development (MIAND), John C. Munro, published a document in August 1982 entitled "The Elimination of Sex Discrimination from the Indian Act." The document outlined the advantages and disadvantages of several models for a solution to the problem. The government generally uses this kind of "nonobligatory" document to make known what it is prepared to yield and what not.

First, reads the text, one may ask to whom the power will be granted to define the new Indian status. Four solutions could be considered: (1) In the first, the bands would themselves each decide who would be members of their group and determine Indian status for themselves. In this case, the option would be for local solutions, and each band would determine its own admission criteria. The government, however, stipulated that these criteria may involve no discrimination between men and women. Some bands, the text states, would probably opt for the criterion of biological descent, others for a cultural criterion, and still others for a combination of the two. When the Indian groups themselves decide, then an authority must be established to which one could appeal against the decision of the band. Under the present regulations, this could be the court.

(2) Under a second solution, the bands would decide on the criteria for membership but the government would specify the rights and duties of the members of the respective bands. This, according to the text, would give the government an instrument with which it could control its own expenditures. The Indians could artificially inflate their numbers if they desired, but the government was not planning to increase the budget of the MIAND substantially. What the Indians are today receiving would later have to be divided among a greater number of members of the respective bands.

(3) A third possibility outlined in the document was that the bands themselves would decide whether they wanted to determine the question of status and membership at all. Each band that chose not to do so could leave the relevant decisions to the government.

(4) Finally, according to the document, the entire matter could be left to the government, and the present situation could be continued. The government itself would then have to take measures to eliminate sexual discrimination from the Indian law.

In a subsequent section, the text of the minister indicated that a number of complicated matters had to be dealt with, whoever made the decisions. To begin with, there are the consequences of marriage with a non-Indian husband or wife. One could allow both Indian women and Indian men who marry a non-Indian to retain their rights and grant no rights to the non-Indian spouse. This solution contains no difficulties for couples who decide to live off the reservation. In the case of divorce or death of the non-Indian spouse, the Indian could return to the reservation. Difficulties, however, arise if the couple decides to live on the reservation. There are various possibilities: the spouse that comes from the outside could be granted a limited number of rights without becoming a member of the band, such as the right to lifelong participation in the family property and the right to live in the family house until death without the non-Indian spouse being able to transfer this property to his or her heirs. With a divorce, the rights of the non-Indian spouse would be annulled. In order to give citizens the opportunity to have their say in policy one would want to grant to the non-Indian spouses the right to participate in elections of the band council, and even to stand as candidates for an office.

These proposals, the text has it, would encounter opposition from the bands, which would feel their culture, values, and traditions threatened by the presence of non-Indians on the reservation. If this proposal, were, nevertheless, implemented, one would have to accept that governmental services on the reservation would diminish in quality, since a larger number of people would have to be administered with approximately the same budget.

I will return to this passage of the ministerial text later. For now, let me note that it was not proposed to grant Indian status to non-Indian men or women who married Indians, which, at least theoretically, would also be a way of making the sexes equivalent.

Various possibilities are available to the children who result from mixed marriages. One is that these children would not be granted Indian status but that they could live with their parents until they reached the age of 21, whereupon, as adults, they would have to leave the reservation. A disadvantage of this, according to the text, is that all kinds of facilities, like schools, would have to be made available for children who were not members of the band. Moreover, the traditions and the cultural uniqueness of bands could be damaged by the presence of a large number of young people who grow up with the realization that they will have to leave the reservation when they are adults. The text then notes that the application of this rule would diminish the number of Indians.

One could also grant all children born of a mixed marriage the status of Indian. This would result in a continual increase in the number of Indians. There would be 140 more after 1 year; 7,700 more after 10 years, and 80,564 more after 40 years. The bands, in this case, would have to take care of an ever-expanding population. Moreover, these people, particularly on reservations where a large number of non-Indians already live, could endanger the preservation of the Indian culture and traditions.

A third possibility would be to specify that the child must have at least 25% "Indian blood" to be recognized as an Indian. The calculation of this percentage can be done in various ways. These calculations would turn out to be very complicated. One would, in fact, recognize *socially* as 100% Indian anyone who had at least 25% Indian blood in his or her veins. The minister's text does not mention this, but it is clear that the number of "Indians" would increase spectacularly in this way. One "full-blood" Indian grandfather or grandmother on either side would suffice for a person to be recognized as an Indian.

Finally, equalization would have to be achieved for illegitimate children of men and women. The present legislation stipulates that an illegitimate child of an unmarried Indian woman acquires the status of Indian unless it can be proven that the father was not an Indian. The illegitimate child of an Indian man and a non-Indian woman, however, is not recognized as an Indian person. The minister proposed to determine the status of these children according to the same modalities as those that apply for legitimate children, which could occur on a voluntary basis or by the action of a court.

The minister proposed that nobody could be emancipated except with his or her consent. This was important, for many people had already indicated that they wanted to recover their Indian rights: women who are married to non-Indians; women who were involuntarily emancipated because their husbands requested it before 1951 (after which the authorities required the consent of both spouses); people who as minors were emancipated with their parents on the request of their parents; people who had lost their Indian status because their mothers and their paternal grandmothers (i.e., on the Indian side) were both non-Indians in origin; and children who had been dropped from the Indian register because it could be proven that their fathers were not Indians. All these people had lost their Indian status involuntarily. In addition, there are still two categories of people who had never been granted the status but who could apply for it: the children born from a marriage between an Indian woman and a non-Indian man and the illegitimate children born from an Indian man and a non-Indian woman. As noted above, tens of thousands of people are involved.

In order to prevent a possible mass reclaiming of Indian identity, the government could impose an artificial limit: the retroactivity of the new law would not go back further than 1976, the year in which Canada ratified the international pact concerning civil and political rights, or to 1951, the year in which the current version of the Indian law was promulgated. Moreover, these rights would only be granted retroactively to people who explicitly requested it. This passage of the text, too, pointed out the large cost such a recovery of rights would involve, the threat to the traditional culture, as well as the social tensions that the reintegration of alien people in a community could engender.

WHO IS WHO? A POWER STRUGGLE

Although the minister's test was presented as a noncommittal document with the purpose of assisting the parties in their considerations, in my opinion, almost all the proposals are intended to reduce the Indian population. The reader is repeatedly informed that the expansion of the Indian population would be detrimental for those who are presently registered as Indians, since the limited resources that are now applied for fewer persons would have to be used for a larger mass. Indian status would have to be adapted in such a way, and the programs that have been developed to benefit the Indians would have to be transformed to such an extent, that the same amount of money and services would have to satisfy (or *not* satisfy) equally the expectations of all those who acquire Indian rights. In fact, the registered Indians are being encouraged, in their own interest, to refuse Indian status to outsiders. The minister also warned that the importing of non-Indians onto the reservations would dilute the autochthon communities and that they would, in this way, eventually lose their *raison d'être*.

All in all, the Indians have been given two choices: to continue to exist on a small scale and with slower expansion than is now the case or to expand a great deal but to live with fewer resources and eventually to merge into and be absorbed by the mass. The proposal of the minister made it clear that the money that Canada will devote to the Indians will not grow by very much, no matter how the ranks of the registered Indians might increase.

Such discourse, even though it is portrayed as only advisory, was clearly intended to aggravate the tensions between the registered Indians and those who were demanding Indian status. The minister could not have been ignorant of the organizations, throughout Canada, of métis or Indians without status and of women who had lost Indian status who were demanding to be recognized as Indians. The government hopes that most bands will choose to keep their volume as small as possible, and there are numerous indications that this hope will be realized. The richer reservations want to keep the number of their members as small as possible, otherwise they would have to share their comfortable income. Harold Cardinal, a well-known leader from the National Indian Brotherhood, says in his book *The Rebirth of Canada's Indians* (1977) that he finds it scandalous that so many members of richer reservations are only concerned with dropping as many members as possible from their band lists in order to increase their personal share in capital and profit.

By the same token, it is also obvious that many people are demanding Indian status explicitly to acquire more material advantages. This can appear to be fraud in the eyes of those who fear they will have to share the little they do have. Fernand Chalifoux, chairman of the Alliance Laurentienne de Métis et Indiens sans Statut, stated frankly in an interview:

> Our object was to group the people of Indian origin from the Quebec region. The most important goal was also to promote economic development, that is, education, housing, jobs, in short, economic development in general. One may not forget that the population of métis and Indians without status in Quebec and Canada has the lowest level of schooling of the entire country, lives in the worst housing conditions, suffers the most alienating pressure, and has the highest rate of imprisonment because of criminal activities. In some places, the unemployment in our community runs to between 65% and 75%. (Gendron, 1982: 115)

It should be obvious that the groups that present themselves in this way to the public at large, even though the data cited are perhaps not totally accurate, are aiming at economic advantages. This same leader admits that relations with registered Indians are not easy. They have very little to share, he notes, and are thus not predisposed to do so.

The Alliance Laurentienne was founded in 1972. Only descendants of Indians can vote or serve in executive positions. The alliance keeps its ranks "pure" in order to be able to claim its rights with a better chance of recognition. The association wants land and rights comparable to those of the registered Indians (Gendron, 1982: 116).

From my fieldwork in the late 1970s and the early 1980s, relations among the métis, the nonstatus Indians, and the registered Indians in the Province of Quebec did not seem good. An important Quebec Indian leader commented to me: "I think it's absolutely absurd for one or another woman [a nonstatus Indian] to be given the right to a free telephone because there was an Indian somewhere in her distant ancestry." The relations between these groups are further complicated, at least in Quebec, by the attitude the province has taken with respect to them. The provincial government has, for its part, manifested much goodwill toward the métis and the nonstatus Indians. Chalifoux, the chairman of the métis organization mentioned above, and another leader of a similar, competing association publicly declared that "the province" considered them favorably. The province, for example, agreed that the members of their associations need pay no more taxes than the registered Indians on the condition that they lived on a reservation (Gendron, 1982: 119–120). Several people from the Indian population told me flatly that the province played the métis off against the Indians:

> The métis are given everything that we have been asking for for years without getting it. These people are being encouraged to come and live on the reservations, even though it is known that there is no room for them. So when we cannot grant their requests for lack of room, the blame falls on our shoulders.

The relations between the registered Indians and the associations of people who demand Indian rights are further complicated by the heterogeneous composition and the artificially elevated volume of some of these organizations. Thus, the Association des Métis et Indiens hors réserve du Québec, which was also founded in 1972, the same year as the alliance, has about 15,000 of the 30,000 people who claim Indian rights within the borders of Quebec. On closer inspection, this association appears to be very broadminded in its specification of the criteria for membership. Not only does it accept women of Indian origin, it allows their white husbands to be full members. Their children are recognized to the third generation. This is one of the reasons why this association has not merged with the alliance. Indeed, the chairman of the alliance speaks very pejoratively about this "sister organization" (Gendron, 1982: 116).

At present, therefore, not only is there competitive tension between registered Indians and those who want to be recognized as Indians, but divisiveness also reigns in the ranks of the latter. The registered Indians fear that their rights will be diluted if the members of the alliance should become their allies, and the alliance fears that its chances will diminish should it join with a sister association in which the "degree of purity" of Indianness is suspect.

All of these relations were placed under further pressure by the obligation imposed by the federal government on itself to implement equal rights for men and women by 1985. This elimination of discrimination concerned, of course, all Canadian citizens and was a question that attracted a great deal of attention. Paragraph 15.1 of the Charter of Rights and Freedom of the Constitutional Act 1982 (Gendron, 1982: 118) recognizes the equality of everyone before the law, without sexual discrimination. Many Indian leaders and Indian groups were accused of being antifeminists because they did not immediately want to agree with equal rights for men and women. In a publication of the Province of Quebec, for example, it was mentioned in a rather neutral tone that the Indian leader, Max Gros-Louis, tried to refute charges in public that he was antifeminist before a women's group (*Rencontre* 2(4), 1981: 5). The so-called antifeminism of the Indian leaders can also be conveniently used as a means of pressure by the associations of métis and nonstatus Indians, which many Indian women who have lost their rights have joined. It was not mere chance that the Association des Métis et Indiens hors réserve du Québec and the Association des femmes autochtones collaborated organizationally (Gendron, 1982: 118). In the early 1980s, the group relationships, the demands of the métis associations, and the demands formulated in the name of equal rights for men and women were partially overlapping. Thus, a modus vivendi had to be found that would satisfy most of the bands as well as the métis and the nonstatus Indians and that would also concur with the stipulations of the Charter of Rights and Freedom, which granted women equal rights.

From the above, it appears that the Indian Law in its successive versions has failed to achieve its objective in various senses of the word. For a considerable time, the law has been able to suppress the number of registered Indians by means of various stipulations, but it also produced social categories of people who feel discriminated against and who, in what is for them a favorable economic climate, are making known their demands again and with more force than previously (see the Indian publications cited in the references section of this work).

THE CULTURAL NATURE OF BIOLOGICAL DESCENT

I would like to go somewhat deeper into the already partially interpreted factual material with an approach that focuses on the process of ethnogenesis. Over the years, and particularly since the introduction of the more restrictive stipulations of the Indian law, all of the parties involved have proceeded from a generally accepted underlying principle: the whites and the Indians are two populations that are physically distinct, two "races." These two races can be mixed, which results in the creation of "half-breeds" in the first mix, "quarter-breeds" in the second, and so on. A person can have 25% Indian blood and still be "Indian." These popular concepts of race were generally accepted in the nineteenth century, the heyday of racist–scientific thought (Banton and Harwood, 1975; Littlefield, Lieberman, and Reynolds, 1982: 641–647; Salmon, 1973). In the past, even some autochthons have used these terms (see Owram, 1982: 315–336 regarding the métis of Riel), which did not then carry the pejorative connotation they have now acquired in more sophisticated circles.

In the discussions and disputes that developed around Indian status, all of the participants accepted the idea that physical filiation was an important *fact*, a *given* that nobody could undo. That I am the son or daughter of this particular man or that particular woman was understood to be, for me and for society, a significant piece of data. Even today, all parties assume, implicitly or explicitly, that physical filiation determines the group of people to which one belongs. Full-blood Indians *belong* among full-blood Indians and not among whites. This belonging is also perceived as a *natural* phenomenon. Nobody questions that a child, *by nature*, enjoys the same status as its parents; the child is assigned socially to the same category of people to which its parents belong.

There is another principle about which the whites and the Indians are in agreement: the higher the degree of purity of the biological filiation, the greater the force of the claim that one can make in the sharing of the rights of the forebears to whom one refers. Expressed in popular terms: people with more Indian blood than other people also have more rights to inherit what their ancestors, the former Indians, have left behind. In addition, full-blood Indians are more authentic than half-breeds. By *being* pure, they have more right to respect. They *are*, in all aspects of their being, more *integral*. These principles are the foundation for statements by both Euro-Canadian parliamentarians and members of Indian groups.

These principles are not always applied consistently. When Indian leaders or Indian spokespeople speak in public, as Indians, they speak about "our ancestors," "our ancestral customs," "our lands," "the lands of our ancestors," suggesting that they have descended from pre-Columbian Indians and from nobody else. They call up the emotional, "natural" bond that they, according to their own norms, feel with respect to those who have given them life. But many of these speakers could, with just as much right, say that their ancestors were "French" and that they themselves were French, if they wished to invoke the biological foundation of their ethnic belonging. According to the law on Indians, one either is or is not an Indian: one cannot be half Indian, or a fourth Indian, or an eighth Indian. They may try to undermine the position of an opponent by telling an outsider that the opponent's wife is actually a pure Canadian who is forced to dye her hair black because it is in her husband's interest to have her "pass" as an Indian.

Even Indians themselves may use the "degree of biological purity" as a basis for prestige, or for the authenticity of claims that one can make for rights. One Indian told me that there were no longer any "real Indians" on the entire reservation. He could not get along on his reservation and spent practically all of his adult life away from his band.

It was not always this way. The formulation in 1850 of the first legal specifications regarding Indian status was lenient in the extreme: anyone who had an Indian father *or* an Indian mother *or* was married to an Indian *or* who had lived with Indians for a long period of time was an Indian. Thus, anyone who formed part of an Indian community in one way or another received the right to be recognized as an Indian.

Almost immediately thereafter, in 1851, the formula was restricted in Lower Canada: non-Indian husbands no longer were considered Indians. The broader definition continued to be applied in Upper Canada but, after the two parts of Canada were united in 1857, the broader definition was applied in both regions.

In 1869, Parliament made another "cultural" intervention: Indian women who were married to non-Indians became "whites," and the white women who married Indians became "Indian." A child's Indian status followed that of its father. The inconsistency in the legislation would be used as a political and economic weapon more than 100 years later in the 1970s, and is used today by Indian women and their sympathizers. Apparently, it is not biology that determines the relations between people but the power relationships of those who determine what is and is not relevant in nature for the deciding of the social order.

THE INDIAN LAW: BACKFIRING FACTITIOUSNESS

It may be said correctly that the Canadian authorities have illogically linked rights to biological filiation by refusing to the children of the sister what they grant to the children of the brother. But that the respective governments have committed "ethnocide" in this way is less clear. As I have shown above, the Canadian authorities have never been completely restrictive in the definition of who was an Indian and who not. The Parliament, in perfect consistency with the principle of biological purity, could have declared that "half-breeds" are not Indians. It also could have been that a white woman who married an Indian would not have been granted Indian status by the authorities. But that was not done. On the contrary, the determination was rather broad in that an Indian is a person whose father is an Indian, whatever the origin of the mother.

The law on the Indians, perhaps in contradiction to what was intended, reinforced and conserved the ethnic category of "Indian." In fact, many people who were recognized in the nineteenth century as Indians were by then not very "Indian" biologically. Members of the southern reservations of Quebec were so mixed that by 1844–1845, a commission wrote about the Caughnawaga that there were almost no unmixed Indians remaining on the reservation (Jamieson, 1978: 23). (Indians in the isolated North were, of course, less mixed). The legal recognition of "Indian" combined with the reservation system has contributed to the continued existence of Indian groups as such. Nonrecognized Indians and métis have to strive tenaciously to be recognized as a specific group. Indians who are recognized by law enjoy political advantages that are not available to nonrecognized Indians and métis. Indian leaders who reacted in 1969 against the White Paper issued by the MIAND understood the strategic possibilities that Indian status and Indian reservations offered them, even while those same artifacts were symbols of colonization and oppression and a stigma that the white Canadians wanted to eliminate.

The effect of the Indian law has been to make a large number of people *ethnically*—and in the eyes of most people thus also *biologically*—more In-

dian than they in fact are. This enables Indians and Indian leaders to continue their opposition to the acquisition of resources by métis and nonstatus
Indians—even though all three social categories overlap biologically. Indian women who by their marriage with a non-Indian have lost their status
stand, along with their children, on the other side of a barrier to resource
access because of action by the white Parliament.

-3-

THE HURONS OF QUEBEC

THE HURON VILLAGE IN 1968: A NASCENT COUNTERCULTURE

When I first did ethnographic fieldwork among the Hurons of Quebec for six months in 1968, the theories discussed in this book had not yet been published. The initial object of my study was then of a different nature. I had already undertaken long-term fieldwork among the Yaka of Zaire (1961-1965), a people whose culture had only been superficially touched by the colonizing West, and I had had the opportunity to observe the first transformations caused by the contact with the outside world. After that experience, it seemed interesting to study a culture that everyone was saying had virtually disappeared. The frame of reference that oriented the beginning of the research was thus clearly an acculturation paradigm: How do cultural systems react with each other, and, in this particular case, how does a cultural system disappear? How is one culture absorbed into another (Roosens, 1980)?

It soon emerged that my field of research was more interesting than I had expected. For in 1968, the Hurons had begun to create a *counterculture* and had taken the leadership of the Association des Indiens du Québec. After another research period in 1969, and through contact with the initial literature on ethnic phenomena, the Hurons seemed to me to be almost a textbook case against which various hypotheses could be tested.

First of all, the situation of the Hurons gave me an opportunity to look for an answer to the following question: What are the differences and the similarities between the past as it is described by historians and the past as it is presented by members of an ethnic group? In their militant posture, the Hurons continually reached back into their past to validate their political positions, and a large number of historical sources, beginning with the *Relationes* of the Jesuit missionaries of the seventeenth century (e.g., Jones, 1909; Tooker, 1964), were available that made possible a comparison of what the Hurons were saying about themselves.

Second, it was relatively easy to investigate the relationship between ethnic group formation and the physical characteristics of the group: The Hurons had been mixing for three centuries with the French and other foreigners so that none of the residents of the Huron Village could be identified by an outsider as being phenotypically Indian.

Third, the Hurons differed only minimally from the culture of the surrounding French Canadians. This gave me the opportunity to investigate the connection between objective cultural differences and similarities, on the one hand, and ethnic portrayals of cultural differences, on the other.

When I first studied the Huron Village in 1968, I found a community squeezed into a very small area. One could hardly speak of the Huron as having their own territory, and hunting was only a sporadic activity. Virtually all the men were completely absorbed into the "modern" economic sector, with many working off the reservation in Canadian companies and institutions. Of the 979 Hurons who were listed on the register in 1966, 471 lived permanently off the reservation (Morissonneau, 1970), and some even lived in the United States.

The ancestry of all the inhabitants of the Huron Village indicated a strong degree of mixing with non-Indians. All the family names of the Hurons except for one—Sioui, probably a transformation of Siweit—sound very French: Bastien, Duchesneau, Dumont, Gros-Louis, Lainé, Laveau, Paul, Picard, Savard, Vincent.

Most of the other dimensions of the precolonial culture have also completely disappeared. Today, the Hurons no longer know their language. The last Huron who could speak it died at the beginning of this century. One registered Indian, who, incidently, did not live on the reservation, had been able to obtain a copy of a French–Huron dictionary that had been compiled by the Jesuit missionaries. No grammar was available. I sought in vain for traces of the former religion and of the traditional family system.

Yet of all the Indian groups, this was the one that, in the late 1960s, had militantly taken the leadership of the Association des Indiens du Québec, which comprised approximately 30,000 Indians on 50 reservations. More particularly, the grand chief of the Hurons, as the secretary-general of this association, played a leading role and regularly spoke, in hard and demanding terms, about the rights of Indians on radio and television broadcasts. The grand chief was familiar with the world of the whites: French was his mother tongue, and he was married to a woman who descended from a white father and an Indian mother. Although he had opponents on his own reservation, all the registered Indian men, with few exceptions, spoke this militant language to outsiders.

Moreover, these Indians had set out deliberately to develop a Huron *counterculture*. When I compared the characteristics of this neo-Huron culture with the culture depicted in the historic records, most of the modern traits, virtually everything, were "counterfeit": the folklore articles, the hair style, the mocassins, the "Indian" parade costumes, the canoes, the pottery, the language, the music. There is one thing, however, that all these constructed cultural characteristics have in common: they represent attempts to introduce a perceptible difference between the Hurons and the surrounding Canadians in a way that suggests some Indian stereotype. More than mere symbols are involved here. As we will see, it is with regard to what they call their territorial rights that the Hurons are most ethnically militant.

I will next summarize how some of the most authoritative historians have pictured the culture of the Hurons. That picture will then be contrasted with what an Indian leader presents as the historical truth in his political discourse and his writings. Then, from my own fieldwork, I will describe what the average resident of the Huron reservation considers to be the reality among the Indian peoples in Canada. The hard sociographic facts that have been assembled and published by a study commission for the national government provide a further useful contrast to the other pictures. I will thus compare "subjective" with "objective" history, and "subjective" with "objective" culture, in order to show how ethnogenesis proceeds—how people feel themselves to be a people and how they continue to maintain themselves as such, if necessary in the face of contrary "facts."

A HISTORIAN'S VIEWPOINT

Now and then, people in Huron Village discuss and remember the dismantling of their culture by outsiders. Indeed, professional historians talk about the facts in the same basic tone, for the Hurons do have a tragic past. They picture themselves as a victimized people, and their belief in this picture is not based on some distorted ideology.

The Hurons, then called the Wendat, seem to have prospered until the first half of the seventeenth century, when they encountered the French. In a short time they were decimated by disease, slaughtered by the League of the Iroquois, and chased out of their villages. Then came 250 years of living in protective status, on land that was later taken from them. The Hurons ended up, in the first decades of this century, with a tiny reservation area, the size of a miniature village.

For a thorough presentation and analysis of the history of the Hurons up to 1660, I refer to the work of Trigger, *The Children of Aataentsic* (1976).

Here, I will only sketch in broad lines two contrasting themes. The first is that the Hurons were victims of the whites, especially the French: their language, culture, land, and houses were taken by the French, and the Jesuits played a particularly important role in this. This is the theme most cited by Hurons. The second theme is that the Hurons were the victims of other Indians, namely of the Iroquois (and among them the Mohawks), whose descendants now live on the reservation of Caughnawaga near Montreal, and that the Hurons of Lorette have the "French" to thank for their survival.

The Huron language was related to those of the peoples of the Iroquois League, and is classified by linguists as Iroquoian. This relationship with the language that was spoken by the five peoples of the League, however, is rather weak, so that close relations between the Hurons and the Iroquois are assumed to be situated in the remote past. It is certainly *not* the case that the Hurons were one of the Iroquois peoples just before the arrival of the French in America.

At first contact with the colonizers, the Hurons appear to have been a people composed of four tribes: the Attingawantan, the Arendarhonon, the Attigneenongnahac, and the Tahontaenrat, who largely lived independently of one another (Trigger, 1976: 30). The Hurons, in the first half of the seventeenth century, were strongly established in an area near Lake Simcoe (Trigger, 1976: 28-29). They were a sedentary people, although a secondary but important source of income was hunting in the winter, mostly by the men. The Hurons, therefore, were not hunters like the Montagnais, the Attikamek, or the Naskapi in the North or the Algonquins of the East.

Trigger has convincingly demonstrated that the Hurons occupied an important place in the pre-Columbian economy of the Indian peoples, for the Hurons lived in a climate and on land that permitted a surplus production of corn. This food was exchanged for game with peoples who were primarily dependent on hunting and fishing, so there was already a trading network before the arrival of the whites. The barter trade became very extensive with the fur trade in the seventeenth century. Although a "European phenomenon," it used the already existing circuit and trade routes. As appears in detail from the recent work of Martin, *The Keepers of the Game* (1978: 175-176), the Hurons were not the first or the only trading partners of the French fur trade: the Mic-Mac, the Montagnais, and the Abenaki were involved in this barter trade much earlier than the Hurons, and had become more dependent on and thus involved in the European capitalistic system much earlier than the Hurons.

Initially, the Hurons were not very interested in trading with the whites.

It was primarily the French who skillfully stimulated this trade by creating bonds of friendship, the celebration of meetings, and the exchange of ''tribe members,'' who for a time came to live among the people they were friendly with. Gradually, commercial relations grew, and the Hurons came to play an important role as a sort of broker (Trigger, 1976: 244–245): the Hurons used their traditional relations with the hunting peoples and acted as intermediaries between the northern and western Indians and the French. At that time, it was a generally accepted custom that one did not cross the territory of neighboring peoples without permission (Trigger, 1976: 214) and that passage required payment of a toll *in natura* on goods that were transported through another's territory. We thus have a scenario that reveals the Wendat as a people who lived predominantly in peace with most of the neighboring peoples. This does not mean, of course, that there was a kind of ''common market'' whereby everything would simply be divided among the Indians under a kind of primitive communism. Rather, it was the case, within a ''tribe'' (and certainly within a lineage where members generally lived together in one or more adjacent long houses), that material goods were owned communally and that a degree of hospitality unknown to the Europeans was practiced toward all outsiders. But all Indians do not live together peacefully, by any means (Trigger, 1976: 236).

Relations were always tense between the Wendat and the members of the Iroquois League, even before the coming of the whites (Trigger, 1976: 159, 164). Traditionally, the Wendat would raid the Iroquois with small groups of warriors, and the Iroquois did the same for their part. Although the number of lives taken in these confrontations was small and the ''wars'' were on a small scale, there was a pronounced enmity between them, at least periodically. Men confirmed or raised their status by killing enemies and particularly by taking prisoners. Often, these prisoners were tortured, and torture was practiced by both the Iroquois and by the Wendat. A prisoner was generally incorporated into the family of the warrior who had captured him. By the time he arrived at this new village, his fingernails had already been torn out and a few of his fingers, those used in shooting a bow, may have been torn or bitten off. Sometimes his life was spared. But often he was slowly tortured to death by the members of the community, thus being given the opportunity to die heroically (Trigger, 1976: 70, 73–75, 145). These practices were firmly established and formed an important part of the community life. They were appreciated by everyone, and even the Jesuits never dared to oppose them, even though they were revolted by the practices.

It is important to note—and these are established facts that permit no ideological interpretation on the part of the historian—that hostility existed between the Wendat and the Iroquois before the arrival of the whites. Moreover, there was a system of relationships in force that involved collective property rights of groups and implied the defense and preservation of one's own territory and property.

The profit-oriented fur trade activated these existing relationships. The logic of European trade, and particularly the competition between the Dutch, who were established in the Hudson region, and the French of Quebec, certainly contributed to the confrontation that led the Iroquois to massacre the Hurons in 1649–1650. One must avoid the simplistic interpretation, however, that this decimation was solely the fault of the greedy Europeans.

The Indians were much attracted to the objects offered by the Europeans as trade goods: copper kettles, iron axes, iron knives, clothing, and the like (Trigger, 1976: 221, 412, 429). Had the Indians not wanted these goods, no trade would have been possible, for neither the French nor the Dutch had sufficient military resources to force the local population to produce fur. One may say that the Indians were seduced or that they were lured into trade, and that they were not compensated properly for their labor. Or, one may say that the Indians had no idea of the profits that European traders obtained from the fur trade. But one may not say that the Indians were coerced to engage in trade in the first phase of contact. Later, of course, Indians were coerced to "sell" immense territories by treaties to the colonizers for ridiculously low prices—in some cases, payment was defined as a few flags, some new suits of clothing for the chiefs, a few hundred meters of rope, and some specified number of barrels of gunpowder per year.

On balance, a people like the Wendat could have easily gotten along in the seventeenth century without the French, and it is also true that the Hurons of that era were not *forced* to do anything whatsoever by the French. The Hurons agreed to the barter trade because they thought they could profit by it. They made decisions themselves, as adults within their own culture. From the *Relationes* of the Jesuits it is abundantly clear that the Wendat were not at all helpless and weak "savages," even though they were officially called *sauvages* up to the beginning of the twentieth century, as were all other Indians in Canada.

I am not implying that the French bear no guilt or blame for what happened later to the Wendat. I do want to make clear, however, what I consider to be the fundamental dynamic here: the technology of the West, both its techniques of production and its products, has an intrinsic attraction to all people and ultimately involves people in a global system from which they cannot escape. Whether this is to the benefit of humanity or not is another question.

On the other hand, it would be simplistic to reduce everything that occurred to the Hurons to this one factor. The French used every means possible to start and increase the fur trade. They forged bonds of friendship with the Hurons and brought several Hurons to France as guests. One Huron even went to study at a Jesuit school in France. In exchange, the Wendat accepted the presence of Jesuit missionaries on their territory. The Hurons could hardly have known what they had begun, but the tradition among friendly Indian peoples made it almost obligatory for the Hurons to offer hospitality to the members of the religious order. Ironically, the fate of many Hurons after the attacks of the Iroquois depended on the Jesuits (Trigger, 1976: 327, 330, 365).

During the early seventeenth century, the cultural influence of the West was channeled to the Hurons by the Jesuits in the area around Lake Simcoe known as "Huronia" (Trigger, 1976: 398–399). In missionary history, the Jesuits of centuries ago were cited as a textbook example of adaptation to the culture of the peoples among whom they worked. Unlike their predecessors, the Franciscans (one of whom had worked among the Hurons before the Jesuits took over the sector), the Jesuits worked to achieve a certain accommodation: they learned the Huron language and compiled a dictionary, and they tried to gain insight into and describe the customs of the Hurons. The Jesuits were, in principle, not in favor of bringing the Hurons into frequent contact with the other French. The missionaries believed that the Indians would not meet many good behavioral examples among the French adventurers (Trigger, 1976: 468).

On the other hand, any customs that the Jesuits found to run counter to the doctrine of the Catholic church were to be eliminated. The missionaries were unhappy with the superstition and magical practices, with the creation story of the Hurons, with the sexual licentiousness of the youth before marriage, and, of course, with the great ignorance of the Hurons with regard to the "true religion." As Trigger (1976: 512, 530, 534) shows, it is impossible to remove certain institutions, belief contents, customs, and practices without touching the system as a whole. But it took many years before the Jesuits discovered that the cultural system of the Hurons formed a complex whole of which the elements were all interrelated. In the meantime, they tried to convert people and to baptize the dying—if need be in secret against the will of relatives. They refuted the beliefs of the Hurons in public meetings, and it took a long time before the Jesuits grasped the cultural characteristic of the Hurons to allow everyone to have his say, to listen to one another with attention, and to believe what one wanted, even while listening attentively to others.

There were a series of public conversions among the Hurons, and some who worked for the new religion suffered for it (Trigger, 1976: 547, 549). After a while, organized opposition arose against the Jesuits with the explicit charge by the "traditionalists" that the Jesuits were trying to dismantle the customs and ancestral traditions of the Hurons on which the well-being of the people depended. The traditional healers, soothsayers, and ritual specialists, who, in the eyes of the Jesuits, were the bearers of anti-Christian superstition, remained the missionaries' enemies for years.

It is difficult to determine the degree to which the presence of the Jesuits and their activity contributed to the growth of the fur trade, but it is probable that they encouraged the Hurons to trade regularly with the French. This does not mean that without the Jesuits the Hurons would never have become so dependent on the French, or that they never would have attracted the envy and competition of the Iroquois (which would have spared them the rest of their catastrophic history) (Trigger, 1976: 622, 626, 629, 653).

The Iroquois League, and more particularly the Mohawks, competed fiercely with the Hurons, their traditional enemies, within the trade network that had developed with the introduction of the European market economy. In their trade relations with the Dutch, they were encouraged, as were the Hurons by the French, to exchange as much fur as possible for imported goods. The Iroquois probably became more dependent than the Hurons on trade with the outside world because, unlike the Hurons, the Iroquois did not have fertile agricultural land, so their subsistence was less secure. However that may be, the Iroquois increasingly took control of the trade routes from the Huron country to the region of modern Quebec and tried to capture as much as possible. Their attacks on the trade traffic became so intense that trade with the French virtually ceased in some years (Trigger, 1976: 644). Although the survival of the Hurons was not immediately threatened by the cessation of this trade, their trading partnerships with the peoples to the northeast and west were.

How it happened nobody knows, but in 1649 and thereafter the Iroquois began to attack Huron villages in such a way that the population could only either flee or be slaughtered. The progress of these events was recounted by the Jesuits in some detail. The position of the Hurons in their own region soon became untenable. Some fled to the West and took refuge with friendly groups; others were integrated by their enemies who had laid their land waste; still others fled to Quebec. What happened after the dispersal of the Hurons from their region around Lake Simcoe seems to me to be remarkable.

A portion of the Hurons fled to the West and there joined the Ottawas with whom they merged. Another group went over to their archenemies, the Iroquois, and another went to Quebec.

Trigger (1976: 769–770, 783–784) estimates the number who went to the Iroquois at a few thousand, in any event a much larger number than the 300 who moved to Quebec. The Mohawks, the Onondaga, and the Seneca urged the Hurons—after burning many Huron villages—to come and settle with them. Promises were made that the Hurons would be treated as brothers and sisters. Probably the best interpretation is that the Iroquois wanted to strengthen demographically their greatly reduced ranks by the assimilation of another people. It was completely in the tradition of these Indian groups that captured enemies would take the place of family members who had been killed in battle. The family could decide to torture the prisoner to death, but this was not inevitable: if the prisoner adapted well to the new situation, his life could be spared and he could even be adopted as a respected member of the family.

Under this threat of life or death, many Hurons successfully assimilated into the Iroquois. From the Jesuit missionaries active among the Iroquois that we know, after about a generation, the Huron language had died out and nothing remained of the Huron identity among the Iroquois. By marriages and forced acculturation, the Hurons were absorbed. Assimilation was also made easy because the two cultures were similar in a number of respects. And though nothing is known about the motivation of the Hurons, the facts show that they preferred to put themselves in the hands of the Iroquois with all the attendant dangers than to join the French, their allies. Historical data (Trigger, 1976: 784) indicate that many contacts took place later between the assimilated Hurons and the group that had settled near Quebec. The historical sources also mention that a number of "Iroquois" came to live among the Hurons of Quebec. These were probably assimilated Hurons. This could also explain, for example, why the grandfather and the father of the Grand Chief Max Gros-Louis, on the basis of oral tradition, told their children that they were originally from the Onondaga, one of the Iroquois peoples, and why Gros-Louis today has the Hurons "descend" from the Iroquois.

The Wendat group that fled to Quebec is still in existence with its own identity and can claim an unbroken ethnic tradition: as a people with its own identity they knew no interruptions, and, although their own culture in many respects has disappeared, it has not been completely absorbed. A small group of Wendats asked the Jesuit missionaries (who had remained in the region of Lake Simcoe) to have them accepted by the French of

Quebec. The Jesuits, concluding that it was their duty to assure the continued existence of this group, provided for the support of these Hurons, at least in the beginning. This group of Wendats, roughly estimated at about 300 people, were accommodated on the western end of the Island of Orleans (Trigger, 1976: 802–803), where the Jesuits had built their own fortified residence. The Indians were given land so that they could support themselves by agriculture. In Sillery, another part of Quebec, there was already a group of Montagnais, also under the guardianship of the Jesuits.

After the Hurons had been settled for a time on the Island of Orleans, they received repeated requests from the Iroquois, both from the Mohawks and from the Onondagas, to come and settle in the land of the Iroquois. The history of these negotiations is too long to be recounted here in detail. A relationship of alternating war and peace developed between the Iroquois and the Hurons, and the Hurons were again decimated by attacks and obliged under physical pressure to accompany the Iroquois back to their country. The French, who observed this happening, did not intervene and so were accused by the Hurons of openly betraying their allies (Trigger, 1976: 804–813). Another group of Hurons, after receiving many promises, reportedly left with the Iroquois only to be murdered underway (Trigger, 1976: 813).

The French authorities finally decided that the Hurons had to be defended. Through the intervention of the Jesuits, and together with Montagnais and other "sauvages," the Hurons were assigned a domain by a grant that was ratified by Louis XIV. The land was expressly allocated to the Indians, but the Indians had to remain on this land under the supervision of the Jesuits. Later, the Jesuits received a grant from the Seigneur de Roberval, who left them an area of 2 miles by 10 (Gérin, 1900: 95). This area largely coincided with that of the Hurons, except for a part that ran along the river. The Jesuits considered the land as theirs and had it registered as such. They petitioned the king to transfer to them the remaining portion of the Huron land, stating that the Indians had left the area for lack of firewood. Gérin (1900) demonstrated that Roberval probably never really owned the land in the first place since he never had it surveyed or registered and transferred to him by the local authorities. Roberval later acquired a still larger area that adjoined his as "compensation" for the parcel he had never really owned (Gérin, 1900: 95).

Gérin's account contains a number of improbabilities. How is it possible to give away land that one does not possess and this with the involvement of a notary? However it may have happened, the Jesuits acquired all the land that had been given to the Hurons. Sillery is near the river where the present *quartier élégant* of Quebec is situated. One way or another the Hurons lost 16 square kilometers of very valuable property.

In the meantime, the Hurons, under the direction of the Jesuits, moved, with a few intermediary stops, to Lorette and settled there in 1697 on the land where they now live. The Jesuits requested even this remaining land in Sillery, claiming that the Hurons had left the area by the river. In 1773, the Jesuits were officially suppressed by an order of the pope. Only then did the Indians learn that their property had been transferred to the Jesuits (Gérin, 1900: 106). The Hurons protested officially to the authorities at the time. This protest phase began in 1791 with a letter, which was published by Gérin.

The protests of the Hurons, who sent representatives to the king of England at the beginning of the nineteenth century, continued tirelessly. A special parliamentary commission reacted positively to the complaint of the Indians (Gérin, 1900: 110), but the advice of this commission was not followed. Finally, the Hurons decided to send a delegation to the king of England, and Chief Vincent was received by him. Vincent's tribal members sent him a letter, which contained the following passage (Vincent, 1978: 23):

> Our joy was complete when we learned of your good reception by His Majesty and his response in our favor. The last letter we received on 24 June mortified us. The poison of our antagonists has insinuated itself into the mind of the Venerable Minister of our affairs, but our rivals cannot prove that we are not the true descendants, but we are without doubt the true descendants of the Hurons of Sillery, our language is the same, it has not changed up to the present, we are Hurons by nation. In our old deeds of Sillery, Kamiskda d'Angachit means in Huron L'Anse Saint-Joseph. We are the heirs of our fathers, the cheating of the Jesuits fooled our ancestors because they were good Christians. The transmigrations of our great-grandfathers forced by the Jesuits are in the same Seigneurie of Sillery, which means that they have always been on our land. When our predecessors left, they settled at Saint-Michel, also called Sainte-Fonge, and then at Ancienne-Lorette, and finally in the village where we are now living.

But the trip to England—not such an ordinary venture in the beginning of the nineteenth century—yielded nothing, and Sillery disappeared for good.

In the meantime, the Indians, partially due to the actions of the Jesuits, had already been culturally assimilated to a large extent. In the *Relationes*, they are described with an enormous amount of praise as very dutiful Catholics who came to church early every day to meditate and attend mass. The Hurons also served as volunteers in the army and fought on the French side. In short, the Jesuits seem to have very soon succeeded in taking control of this small group of Hurons, who were, moreover, totally dependent on them.

It appears from the same sources that the Hurons would go on hunting trips for months at a time: they left at the beginning of winter, returned home at Christmas, and then left again for their hunting grounds. This shows that they did not simply become farmers after the French manner. That the Hurons were to a degree also very active hunters until the beginning of this century has been convincingly demonstrated in great detail by Boiteau in a master's thesis (1954). In evidence of this, Boiteau described a large number of hunting techniques that he learned from the older Hurons.

In the further course of history, the Hurons were given the area of Rocmont by a grant from the government, which then set land apart for the benefit of poor Indians. This hunting area, where the Hurons had built a *cabane d'automne* (autumn lodge), was, after the building of the railroad between Quebec and Lake Saint John, gradually appropriated by a hunting club of millionaires who were mostly from New York. It was then abandoned by the Indians, who were constantly having difficulties with these visitors.

The *quarante arpents* (about 40 acres), the lands given to the Hurons by the Jesuits, were sold at the beginning of this century by a grand chief under suspicious circumstances, as appears from a number of interviews (Boiteau, 1954). Still other pieces of land were sold by "traitors of their own people." Thus, in the 1960s, when their reservation was first described in a scientific way by Morissonneau (1968), the Hurons lived on a "territory" that was very small. To this area a piece of land was added. Through the efforts of Grand Chief Max Gros-Louis, the federal government had purchased it and turned it over to the Hurons in 1968.

There is absolutely no doubt that the Hurons, as disciples of the Jesuits and as allies of the French, were granted land to which they could not claim any ancestral rights. But it is also clear that the same land was taken from them in dubious ways. Thus, the hunting grounds the Hurons used to support themselves were first granted them and then again taken away. Strictly speaking, the situation of the Hurons is totally different from that of the Cree, who negotiated with Hydro-Québec and the federal and provincial authorities over the James Bay region. It is also different from that of the Attikamek and the Montagnais. These historical facts have long been known, and the intense activity the Hurons developed in the nineteenth century to regain Sillery prove that they are aware of these historical relations.

A UNITED FRONT

When in the 1960s the united front of the Indians of Quebec was established, the Hurons joined the other autochthons. Max Gros-Louis, Grand Chief of the Hurons, was then secretary-general of this group. Together with the Inuit, the Amerindians then negotiated in 1969 with the Canadian government—I was present at those sessions—in a meeting in a hotel in the city of Quebec. All groups participated at that meeting, and autochthons demanded 85% of the territory of Quebec or 5 billion dollars.

The negotiations were conducted in the name of one united front of autochthons. The leading personalities from the most acculturated and urbanized groups spoke for the people. This was much appreciated by the representatives of the more remote reservations, who could not speak French and knew much less about the negotiation techniques of the white authorities. This same group of leaders also defended the rights of the Cree in the James Bay dispute when Hydro-Québec and other firms, in consultation with the authorities, had begun major projects without consulting the local population.

SPLITTING

The leaders of the Cree and the Inuit gradually lost their confidence in the Association des Indiens du Québec. It is difficult to determine what precisely happened, but the Cree and the Inuit distanced themselves from the other Indians of the association, established their own *grand conseil*, and began to work with their own attorneys. Some Indians of the southern reservations assured me that large bribes were involved in the conclusion of the James Bay Convention and that the provincial government in particular caused a break in the common front of the autochthons. Still others told me the same thing and added that it was said that some members of the southern reservations also received hush money.

Insiders from the northern Indian groups gave me another explanation: the leaders from the North, whose rights were actually at stake, received the impression that the southern reservations, which had absolutely no claim to lands, wanted to turn the negotiations in favor of the Amerindians of Quebec as a whole so that the southern reservations would also benefit. The Indian leaders and their advisors then feared that the negotiations would have less chance of success, since they would have to work with arguments that were less substantial than those of the Cree and the Inuit taken separately. The Indian leaders of the North also did not want the southern reservations, which were materially already better off in comparison with the North, to enrich themselves at their cost. I was also told that the Hurons were considered by the northern Indian groups to be a creation of the colonial period who as refugees had received land from the French in an area that did not belong to them according to their ancestral traditions.

In the recent report on the developments in the James Bay affair written by outsiders working for the government, the same interpretation is given to the fact that the Cree and the Inuit went their own way: they found that the association was not primarily defending their rights but those of the Indians as a whole, while the matter actually concerned the lands of the northern bands. In any event, the members of the association could not agree on how the fruits of the united action would be divided, and in the dissolution of the association the major differences in the degree of acculturation and in the respective histories of the peoples and bands become obvious.

The Attikamek and the Montagnais, for example, decided to distance themselves from the association and together established a grand conseil to negotiate further with the authorities. They believe that they can better defend their own interests, with the assistance of advisors and technicians, because they can present stronger arguments than other groups. In the text they submitted to Premier Lévesque, they left no doubt that they have strong legal and historical grounds for their case ("Nishastanan Nitasinan," 1979). The conclusion of this text reads as follows:

> In the next two or three years, we want to analyze in greater depth the nature of our territorial rights, the past and present use of our lands both by our peoples and by the dominant society, and to prepare the definition of a program of socioeconomic, social, educational, cultural development, and so on. . . . Following the example of several other associations of autochthons before us, we address ourselves to the Government of Canada, acknowledged protector of our rights and interests, to furnish us the financial resources to conduct such studies.
>
> In concluding this memoire, we ask you to ponder the meaning of the words appearing on the title page: NISHASTANAN NITASINAN (our land, we love it and we hold to it).

The Hurons, by contrast, are trying to come into their own and to obtain their rights by accepting the rules applied by their white opponents. The Hurons can advance no noteworthy cultural uniqueness, can make no claim to a mode of production that clearly deviates from the Euro-Canadian, and, in the last centuries, have only possessed lands "given" to them. The Hurons can only argue that they feel cheated and that their land was stolen from them, but these are not solid arguments in the terms of the white negotiators. If the leaders of the more isolated groups, who have a more convincing case, are not prepared to include the Hurons among them, there is probably nothing to be gained, not even compensation for the Sillery lands, the Rocmont lands, the quarante arpents, or the lands where the Laurentides Park is now located and where the Hurons earlier hunted and trapped. "The oldest and most faithful allies of the French" will then have been abandoned to the course of history.

-4-

INDIAN POLITICAL IDEOLOGY AND HARDER FACTS

THE VIEWPOINT OF A POLITICAL LEADER

Max Gros-Louis, the Grand Chief of the Hurons, who will be heard in interviews in a later chapter, published a kind of autobiography in 1972 that also interprets the political position of the Indians: *Le premier des Hurons* (all the references in this chapter are to this book). A second edition was published in 1981, and it has also been published in English. This text offers us the opportunity to examine the relations between the Hurons and the Canadian majority from still another point of view, and to analyze how the concrete political ideology of an Indian leader is structured and how this ideology is related to the information we have gathered from other sources.

In Search of the Truth

Le premier des Hurons is intended to appear to the outsider as a serious work that, for once, finally explains the history of the Canadian Indians as it actually occurred. The author states explicitly that it is not a revolutionary document but an authentic attempt to reconstitute what is true to reality (Gros-Louis, 1981: 11, 13). In the beginning of the book, it is stated that it is published with the financial support of the Conseil des arts du Canada, a national institution that finances scientific research. The book is dedicated to a Swiss professor of medicine and has a foreword from an American professor of literature. In the book itself, there are a great number of citations from professional historians, and the version of the past that Max Gros-Louis brings us is said to rest in the oral tradition of the Hurons (1981: 13, 227, 239–240).

The author adds force to the objective orientation of his work by pointing to the unreliability of a great deal of the history that has been written by white colonists. The "history" as it is taught in the schools, even to the children of Indians, is full of gross misrepresentations and lies, according to the author. Gros-Louis sets out to undo this deception. *Le premier des Hurons* thus demands credibility: it is not a novel or a political program.

Political Inspiration

But if we examine the volume's content in a broader anthropological context and compare it with other sources and with direct field observations, the Gros-Louis volume can hardly be interpreted as anything other than a political product that skillfully offers a broad foundation for the demands of the Indians in general and of the Hurons in particular. The first element that strikes the informed reader is the explaining away of the divisions and the enmity that used to exist between the various Indian groups of what is now Canada. The historical fact that the Hurons were decimated by the Iroquois around the middle of the seventeenth century is veiled throughout: the whites "say" that it happened; the Hurons and the Iroquois are one and the same people (Gros-Louis, 1981: 11, 21, 22): in fact, the Hurons are Iroquois, for the languages of these two peoples were related; or still, the Iroquois are Hurons (p. 17); the father of Gros-Louis was an Onondaga (p. 21), thus an Iroquois; if there was ever enmity between the Hurons and the Iroquois, then this was incited by the French and the English, who set these Indian groups against each other (p. 22).

Nowhere is it said that the Iroquois massacre of the Hurons never took place, but it is insinuated that it is highly exaggerated and that dissension between the Indians is a product of the whites' making. For the author, it is essential that the former hostility between the Hurons and Iroquois be neutralized. Gros-Louis stresses that the Indians have to unite if they want to be restored in honor; he considers it inopportune to recall former hostilities. Moreover, he is married to a woman who, through her mother, is a descendant of the Mohawks of Caughnawaga, an Iroquois group.

The "Natural" Superiority of the "First Cultures"

The former hostilities between Indians are not just minimized. A kind of pan-Indian culture is painted by the author, a culture that unites all Indians against all outsiders and primarily against the whites. The impression is given that the Hurons of Lorette, and certainly the author himself, still possess a large part of some innate Indian culture that clearly distinguishes them from the whites. Gros-Louis does not say this in so many words; he even admits that the Hurons have lost much of their culture (Gros-Louis, 1981: 33, 39, 62, 168, 203, 208–209) and that only dancing and handicrafts remain (p. 168). But in his discussion, he merges his own people so much with the others that these facts are obscured. It is all the easier for the author to do this because he himself is active both on the local level of the Huron Village and on the provincial and national levels, so he speaks in the name of the Hurons and in the name of the Indians of Quebec—and even in the name of Indians of Canada as a whole. The implication is that all Indians share traits that distinguish them from whites.

The first trait is the presumed Indian bond to nature. The Indians know nature, with which they have lived for more than 30,000 years. They respect the plants and the wild animals, in contrast to the colonizing whites who pollute rivers and kill animals purely for pleasure and do not even eat them. Indians are also much more skilled and competent than whites at surviving in nature. Gros-Louis develops this theme strongly as he describes an adventurous journey of five months in northern Quebec. On that journey, he and some other Hurons accompanied two engineers on a mapping expedition. Without the ingenuity of the Indians, these educated whites would probably not have returned. In any case, they were completely disoriented (pp. 77–146).

According to Gros-Louis, Indians in general, like himself, cannot live very long without contact with nature. For himself, office work or a regular job in a factory, like sitting in a school when he was young, were all penances he could not long endure (pp. 147–154). He instinctively turns to hunting and fishing, like the other Hurons who went on the mapping expedition. What the work-obsessed white man can do for a couple of weeks a year while on vacation, the Indians who live in the traditional way can do every day: they can enjoy the natural environment to the fullest. And all Indians could do this if the whites recognized their territorial rights and paid compensation for everything they took and are still taking from the autochthon population (pp. 38–40, 145).

Gros-Louis is of the opinion that the Indians can remain a "young people" if they do not permit themselves to be absorbed by the large cities and the alienated way of life that prevails in them (pp. 180–181). Even the food of the Indians, according to Gros-Louis, is more flavorful and healthier than what the whites eat. Indians live from fresh fish, smoked salmon that they prepare themselves, and from wild animals (pp. 188–189). In this respect, too, the Indian culture is superior. The whites consume degenerate food.

Not only do Indians live in harmony with nature, they are also spontaneously inclined to share what they have with others (p. 206). They do not call this "socialism" or "communism." It is simply a spontaneous urge to share what they have. This was how they reacted to the first French adventurers: the Indians offered them hospitality, which was scandalously exploited by the French (p. 14). In contrast with the whites, Indians are not primarily oriented to profit but are more concerned with emotions and values. For an Indian, his word is his bond. Once he gives his word, he does not go back on it. Max Gros-Louis notes that he experienced this when he was a traveling salesman selling sewing machines. With most whites, it was better to conclude an official contract, otherwise it could happen that the ordered machine would be refused simply because the customer changed his mind and did not feel bound because he had signed nothing. The entire white business world operates on corruption. There is only one law: take what you can get. Unfortunately, some Indians have also been infected by the dollar disease as a result of their contact with white civilization and now must constantly satisfy new "needs."

It is precisely the same with regard to political power: an Indian chief is chosen for his human qualities. He must be a mature person who is detached and disinterested. The conscience of an Indian is not for sale. This is in contrast to what happens in the white world, where politicians get into power by lies and set out intentionally to line their own pockets (p. 169). According to Gros-Louis, this can even be said about certain ecclesiastical dignitaries.

Nor do Indians manufacture murderous weapons at an insane tempo: they are prepared to live in peace in one human brotherhood. Max Gros-Louis even considers it possible to live in harmony with the Quebecers, if they were to properly and truthfully inform themselves about the Indians (p. 241).

Indians are also tolerant about religion. Thus, for example, the Hurons, although they stay faithful to their Catholic rites, understand perfectly well that other people, including Indians, are members of other denominations. This same mildness also appears in the way in which all Indian tribes raise their children: they are not at all strict or dictatorial, and one does not expect the children to accept anything without having experienced it themselves (pp. 169, 171).

The Avid Openness of Indian Culture

That Indians have their own feelings and their own lifestyle in no way implies that they would form a world closed in on itself. Indians are open to all the good things that come from the outside. Gros-Louis professes a great deal of admiration for the sciences that have developed in the world of the whites, and he even adds that he had wanted to become a doctor like one of his uncles but did not have the chance, as he was expelled from school for having hit a brother who had falsely accused him and called him a "damned savage" (*maudit sauvage*) (Gros-Louis, 1981: p. 53). The Indians, however, do not want to accept anything uncritically from the whites: they want to be selective. Thus, Gros-Louis is opposed to production processes that pollute the environment, but he can completely approve of the building of dams to provide energy, at least if approval is asked of the Indians when their land is affected (p. 59). Gros-Louis finds it obvious that Indians, too, make use of inventions like the airplane, and that they turn to modern medicine if it is effective. Indians are even, in some cases, forced to call on modern technology simply to remain competitive. Some handicraft products would be too expensive if they were made completely by hand (pp. 60, 116). At one place in his book, Gros-Louis even complains that the Indians are the least well-off group in Canada, and he expresses this poverty in terms of Western technology: only 4% of them have electricity in their homes (p. 157).

Gros-Louis reminds us that the Indians have given a great deal to the whites. Corn, tomatoes, potatoes, and sunflowers are among the many products from the New World that whites have taken over. And many traditional Indian medicines were used by whites in former times. The Indians also taught the whites how to deal with the cold and how to survive in a brutal climate (pp. 187–189).

"The Archaic Illusion"

The impression is given that "the Indian culture" is truly vital, even among the Hurons, although, as Gros-Louis admits, assimilation has, indeed, occurred, and the detrimental influence of the whites has had its effect on the Indians (Gros-Louis, 1981: 208–209). This Indian culture, which has survived all assimilation attempts, involves a lifestyle that differs sharply from the white lifestyle and surpasses the white culture in a number of respects: on the human and moral level, the Indian culture is of a higher character than that of the constantly hurrying whites, and it is wiser, too. The impression is also given that Indians could go their own way culturally if the whites would only grant them the funds that are theirs by right.

In this discourse, then, a series of phenomena related to Western culture (environmental pollution, the extinction and mistreatment of certain animal species, alienation by individualistic loneliness, anonymity of life in the large cities, the intense rhythm of work, and the cult of achievement) are taken up by Gros-Louis and transformed into their counterimage: the "Indian culture." In other words, Indians automatically have what the whites are searching for. Why, then, should the Indians permit themselves to be assimilated? Gros-Louis neglects to mention that among the Indians—and even among the people of his own band and on his own reservation—there are many who strive to obtain a maximum number of "Western" possessions. Of the total population of 1,050 Hurons that Max Gros-Louis cites for 1968, about 400 lived off the reservation as far away as in the cities of the United States, primarily in order to earn more money. Gros-Louis also leaves out of consideration the social problems that affect many Indian communities. There are reliable statistics on unemployment, alcoholism, and criminality that present a totally different picture of daily life on many reservations (see Chapter 5). In other contexts, the Indian leaders themselves point out these untenable conditions and actually demand equal opportunities with whites. Moreover, Gros-Louis is known in his own community as a good businessman.

In the light of evidence from previous chapters, Gros-Louis presents a one-sided picture of what he considers Indian culture, to put it mildly. Never in his text does he question the phenotypical belonging of the group he represents. He implies that modern Indians are descendants from the pre-Columbian inhabitants of America. He prefers that Indians marry Indians, and notes that he himself married a woman who is the daughter of a Scottish father and a "full-blood" Mohawk mother, as though such marriages and even marriages with a completely white partner were not an everyday occurrence. In fact, the reservation from which Gros-Louis comes and that from which his mother-in-law came are full of people who have whites among their ancestors (p. 71). Here, too, the Indian illusion is maintained for the credulous reader. And the impression is reinforced when the métis are discussed toward the end of the book, as though the people of the reservations, and certainly those of the Huron Village, significantly differed phenotypically from the métis. Actually, on most of the reservations located close to cities the rate of mixed marriages in recent years was one out of two.

At one point Gros-Louis even compares the Hurons to the older peoples of Europe: it takes generations before a line of relatives is accepted as insiders. Gros-Louis mentions that his own father and grandfather still called themselves Onondaga. Among the younger populations of immigrant countries, such as the United States and Canada, things are different: one is accepted much more quickly as belonging. This is another indication of how authentic Indians the Hurons are and how stringently their ethnic borders are guarded.

Ethnic Logic: Horizontal Equality

That the Indians have their own culture does not mean for Gros-Louis that they cannot live on good terms with other peoples and even with people of the Western culture. Thus, he speaks enthusiastically of how, in the 1960s, he performed in Tours and Paris with a Huron dancing group he founded and how hospitably and admiringly they were received by the French. Gros-Louis stresses that his people, in contrast with the Quebecers, really do love the French, and he also stresses that there are whites who have long taken the side of the Indians because of a love for justice. There is even a category of whites who take the side of the Indians once the whites are correctly informed. But there is also another group that continues to disapprove of the Indians. The readiness in principle of the Indians to maintain good relations with the whites, however, does not mean that the Indians will yield their rights (pp. 239–240).

Gros-Louis sees the political situation as follows: the Indians of Quebec are peoples who were placed under protection in the time of the French colonization. The French did the same thing in Madagascar, North Africa, and elsewhere. The English continued this relationship with the Indians when they conquered the French colonies in America. Now that the Indians no longer massacre one another and that the protection of the whites has clearly become superfluous (perhaps Gros-Louis is being ironic here), one must proceed as elsewhere in the colonized world: one must decolonize and return to the Indians what is their due. Gros-Louis holds the position that 85% of the territory of Quebec still belongs to the Indians because they have not relinquished it in any way. If the Indians were to be compensated for everything that was cheated out of them, the debt of the whites would run to 5 billion Canadian dollars (p. 193).

Gros-Louis states that the Indians want to be reasonable. They do not demand that the Canadians who have unlawfully settled on their lands withdraw or that everything should be paid for. But Gros-Louis does demand that the teaching of the history of the relationships between the whites and the Indians be corrected so that it concurs with what did in fact take place. This would cast the Indians in an altogether different light. They would no longer be presented as savages who scalped people (a custom that, according to Gros-Louis, came from the Europeans).

The rights of the Indians to use extensive territories would also have to be recognized and Indians would have to be granted the corresponding hunting and fishing licenses. Moreover, all the property of the Indians should be appraised, and the Indians must be compensated in accordance with the specifications laid down by federal authorities (pp. 193–194). The case of the Indians would certainly be supported by some large nations if it were submitted to the United Nations, Gros-Louis contends (p. 197).

In the course of his book, Gros-Louis gives signs of readiness to come to an agreement with the whites, although he occasionally hints that the Indians would resort to terrorism should they be driven to despair. He adds that the Indians would not normally be inclined to use such measures (p. 230).

Le premier des Hurons is an attempt to qualify the value of the white culture: it has more bad to offer than good. In most aspects of life, the Indian culture is superior. The Indians can thus claim a culture that is at least equivalent to that of the whites. On the moral level, the Indians certainly need not be ashamed: they are victims whose honor must be restored. When one rehabilitates people who have been found innocent, not only do they receive their possessions back again but they are also restored *socially*, as people of equivalent value. Why should Indians be denied such treatment, especially since the whites have cheated the Indians of their lands and have caused them untold suffering?

THE SOCIOECONOMIC CONDITIONS OF THE INDIANS: UNDENIABLE FACTS

Books and documents such as the book by Max Gros-Louis sketch a rather positive picture of the Indian situation: the Indians are militant, they are legitimate creditors, and they have their own past and their own culture that can counterbalance that of the whites. In other words, the Indians need not be ashamed. Their only problem is that they have not obtained their rights. For Quebec alone, this involves interests in a gigantic amount of territory. Such expositions virtually ignore a number of real and factual aspects of the current situation of the Amerindians.

The Fate of Downtrodden Nations: Marginal Dependency

The Canadian federal government has itself issued a number of documents that make obvious the alarming problems on most of the more than 2,200 Indian reservations in Canada (*Les Indiens*, 1980: 3). These government figures agree with those published by independent scholars like Frideres (*Canada's Indians*, 1974). The government has every interest in presenting the situation of the Indians in a favorable light, but the reality is depressing. Reservations located near large cities are generally better off than the more remote reservations. The Hurons in particular are well off in comparison with most other Indian reservations in Quebec.

Roughly 70% of all Indians, however, live primarily from social assistance (*Les Indiens*, 1980: 29). Of those, it has been estimated that 70% are healthy and capable of working. On many reservations more than 50% are unemployed. Alcohol abuse is responsible for approximately 60% of the diseases suffered by Indian populations (*Les Indiens*, 1980: 9, 22). In 1980, it was determined that 11,000 new houses were immediately necessary if the Indians were to be given hygienically acceptable housing. Death by physical violence occurs among the Indians five times more frequently than in the rest of the population (*Les Indiens*, 1980: 3). In the age group between 16 and 24, the suicide rate is six times higher than among the other inhabitants of Canada (*Les Indiens*, 1980: 3). In some provinces, the number of Indians in jail is three times as high as among the other social categories (*Les Indiens*, 1980: 9).

The statistics, when they are available, are not much more favorable for the Indians who live off the reservations—about one-third of the present Indian population. Although Indians themselves do not consider poor housing to be the most serious problem they face, they live in overpopulated, unhygienic accommodations (*Les Indiens*, 1980: 153). And of these "emigrants" of the reservation, approximately 70% live mainly on social assistance from the government. Two-thirds of these people fall under the Canadian poverty line (*Les Indiens*, 1980: 152). The authors of the governmental report see only one explanation for the rather massive emigration to the city: the situation on the reservations is still worse than in the urban centers (*Les Indiens*, 1980: 157).

With these statistics, one is far removed from a romantic presentation that places the Indians in some idyllic, "natural," and harmonious environment. The processes started by contact with the West and colonization seem to be irreversible. There can no longer be a return to a life in nature that would be comparable to that of the precontact Indians. One may or may not find this regrettable. A great deal of evidence provided by Indians and by experts on the occasion of the James Bay lawsuit (Gagnon, 1973: 58–72) showed that even the Cree and the Inuit of James Bay, who are counted among the most isolated autochthon populations of Canada, are dependent for at least half their subsistence on the white outside world. Many basic products and foodstuffs supplied by whites have become part of their daily lives to the point that it would be difficult to do without them. Despite the fact that they are cut off geographically from the outside world, most of these people would not conduct the fierce struggle for survival against the nature that surrounds them when they know that the outside world can (and will) take care of them. Even when the natural environment is rich and relatively undisturbed, so that one could live from it, there seems to be little willingness to do without supplies from the outside. In the James Bay region, after the construction of the dams, where the intervention of the colonizer and of other Canadian population groups has really taken effect, a return to nature is now physically impossible.

The World of White Goods: A Fatal Temptation

The vast majority of modern Indians live in economic dependence on other Canadians, partly because their territories were confiscated and partly because survival would now be impossible without the petroleum lamps, salt, sugar, clothing, tools, and means of transport and communication that are produced by the industrialized civilization and that cannot be produced by these people themselves. In many places, the automobile and the snowmobile are now indispensable; so is traveling by airplane, for that matter. And most of the equipment used for hunting and fishing is purchased from the outside. It is not only the higher practical value of the resources that are imported that bind the Indians to the outside world but also the enjoyment value (beer, liquor, and soft drinks) and the symbolic value as well. Like whites, Indians are impressed by expensive automobiles and value them more than modest compact cars. Access to technology symbolizes knowledge and power, and this, too, prevents turning the clock back.

Cultural Incongruities

Although they may not wish to go back, neither can most Indians and Inuit, on and off the reservations, compete successfully with the surrounding Canadians. In 1980, 60% of the children who came to school for the first time spoke an Indian language, and the great majority of the autochthons lived apart, geographically or socially. They are caught in a vicious Third World cycle of poverty: they have too little schooling to be competitive and, if they do want schooling, they have to divorce themselves from their culture and families. The young feel inferior in an environment in which the adults live off welfare and use alcohol to break the monotony of having nothing to do. Many Indian leaders realize this and state that the *material dependence*, the "support" from the government, has become one of the fundamental causes of evil. Things might be much worse without this support simply because many Indians have neither the desire nor the opportunity to venture into the competitive world outside, unlike so many Asiatic immigrants in the United States, who appear to do so with an astonishing degree of success. These Asiatic immigrants have at least as large a cultural gap to bridge as do the Amerindians. Indians may take the initiative and may receive support from the government to set up a store or a small business, but those ventures typically fail. A good deal of the borrowed money is never repaid, and the loss suffered by the backers is about ten times higher than in other sectors of the Canadian banking world. The failures are so numerous that the government prefers to invest smaller amounts, for which they do not demand repayment, rather than grant larger loans (*Les Indiens*, 1980: 78–79).

The Bypass Fallacy

Through their leaders, the Indians of Canada are trying to obtain as much compensation as possible for the often fraudulent appropriation of their lands by the whites. In not a few cases, the hope is to receive astronomical compensation that would make it possible to live without misery and without having to go through the arduous labor required for successful competition in modern production structures. The James Bay Convention is an example. The Indians who signed this convention surrendered a gigantic asset for much too low a price, 225 million Canadian dollars and a few material and administrative advantages. In the end, they achieved neither financial nor administrative autonomy.

The Practical Limits of Cultural Relativity

The process that is occurring in the James Bay case is very simple: the people who were most actively against the project and who were involved in the negotiations with the whites are also those who are most apt to be considered for leadership positions in the new "autonomous" administrative structure. But this administrative structure receives money from the Canadian government and has to deal with its various departments. This means that the Indians have to learn the administrative and bureaucratic language. They can do nothing else, for it is inconceivable that the Canadian administration would alter its methods for a few thousand Indians, even if such a change of methods were possible (*La négociation d'un mode de vie*, 1979). And, for their part, the Indians have little or nothing to put in the place of governmental administration: there are no "typically Indian" methods of administering a hospital nor is there a "typically Indian" way of bookkeeping or using typewriters.

Former Indian political leaders are thus inevitably thrust into a position of dependence in which they, much more rapidly than previously, have to retrain themselves to function in the structures of the whites. Their administrative function involves frequent contact with white suppliers and officials and includes travel to and periods of residence in the capital or in other administrative centers. The Indian leaders are thus, more than anyone else, transformed culturally and socially from outside and are, in this way, assimilated to a large degree. The more success the leaders want to enjoy in the obtaining of favorable decisions for their people, the more the style and the knowledge of the whites is demanded, and these elements cannot be acquired casually. One *becomes* them, at least in part. In this way, the most enterprising elements of a group are incorporated into the procedural system and, to a degree, into the value and conceptual system of the majority. Politically, most of these people are also neutralized to some extent.

Thus, it seems somewhat naive to argue that the 330,000 Indians could maintain their own life-style or return to their own culture *alongside* the 25 million other inhabitants of Canada, as is insinuated by many passages in recent Indian writings. From recent experiences in black Africa, it may be feared that whoever does not participate on the present world stage will simply disappear. Most of the Indians of Canada could not survive if they were not supported by the government. Of course, one may argue that the blame for this lies with the whites; but this does not enable the Indians of today to survive. Even under a utopian condition in which all Indian groups would be sufficiently compensated by the government so that neither they nor their children would have to work to stay alive, the Indians would still have to be sufficiently educated to manage the capital they would receive.

There is simply no easy way for the Indians to achieve equality, and this equality can only be achieved by the sacrifice of what many Indians today call their culture. Many individual Indians grasp this only too well: some want to obtain realistic support for their objective and try to continue their studies and build a career; others feel the gulf to be too wide and remain frozen in inactivity. The large number of suicides of young people between the ages of 16 and 24 (six times the rate of the rest of the population of Canada) is certainly not unrelated to the prevailing hopelessness. Nor is the alcohol abuse and the criminality.

It seems to me improbable that it is a conscious clinging to certain cultural institutions that accounts for the faulty economic integration of the Indian population. Indeed, a growing number of Indians are occupying administrative posts that are paid for by the government. Where others take the initiative and cover the risks there is no hesitation to become involved in the system. But creative attempts that are crowned with success are fewer, although they do exist. It is probably not mere chance that the reservations of "the South," which are generally located in the vicinity of large cities, have the largest number of people who have gone into business and seem to be getting along well in this environment. The populations of these reservations have been in intensive contact with the world of the whites for generations and have let themselves be culturally assimilated to an extreme degree.

Rhetoric and Facts

There is a great gap between the rhetoric of most of the political leaders and the everyday reality. I was able to note that most of the Indians of the Huron Village are thoroughly aware of this. Indian leaders are not infrequently accused of illicit pursuit of gain and self-promotion. The depressing conditions of everyday life make many Indians too dispirited to become actively involved in the political struggle. What their leaders say is not always felt or thought by the majority. As my interviews show (see Chapter 6), many stand closer to the "facts" than the discourse of the leadership would lead one to assume.

Up to the present, I have considered critically the standpoint of an Indian leader and a number of hard facts. But the surrounding French Canadian political circles also have had their official viewpoint of what it means to be an Indian in Quebec and what rights and duties flow from this ethnic belonging. This white view of the interethnic relations will be discussed in the next chapter.

-5-

"FRENCH" EXPERTISE AND "FRENCH" AUTOCHTHONY

THE DORION COMMISSION

The Province of Quebec appointed its own "independent" commission in the 1960s to investigate what obligations Quebec had to the Indians and the Inuit. In the late 1960s, the actions of the Association of Indians of Quebec and of other Indian groups elsewhere in Canada had become so visible and the demands of the Indians had been formulated so concretely that the government could do nothing other than react to them.

The final version of the bulky report of this commission, often called the "Dorion Commission" after the principal author of the document, seems to have been written only in 1970 as it takes account of the reaction of the Indians to the White Paper of the minister of Indian Affairs, published in 1969. The first part of Volume 4 of the report, *Le domaine indien*, explains in more than 400 pages the situation as perceived by the members of the Dorion Commission (*Rapport des commissaires*, 1971). The document is written in a bland, unemotional style that is clear and virtually devoid of jargon. My discussion of this report will deal both with its content and with its logic.

Indian Rights: Some Evidence

The Dorion Commission concludes firmly that the Province of Quebec has entered into obligations with respect to the Indians, that the province has not yet met these obligations, and that it will have to do so in the near future. This is the case, notwithstanding the complicated question of the status of the various "reservations" or of the "settlements" that cannot be officially considered reservations and the vagueness with which the so-called "Indian Territory" is described in the various official documents. The Province of Quebec clearly owes the Indians something, even when the claim is judged according to the norms of a Euro-Canadian jurist (Rapport Dorion, 1971: 364).

What are popularly (and also in administrative practice) called "the reservations" of the Indians of Quebec are, in fact, territories with different statuses and different origins. They are areas "reserved for" the benefit of Indians; most inhabitants are registered as Indians with the appropriate department of the federal government, and registered Indians on reservations enjoy special legal status in Canada. But the common character of reservations ceases at this point.

Some of these reservations existed, in whole or in part, long before the first "Indian law" was passed in 1851, as is the case for a part of the Huron reservation, which, like Caughnawaga (or Kanawakhe) was established by or through the intervention of the Jesuits. Other reservations were formed by the Province of Quebec and will revert to the province when the last resident leaves the reservation. In 1970, there was a reservation on which only a single person lived. For its part, the federal government has, on occasion, purchased land on behalf of some Indian groups. This is the case with the Hurons, to whose reservation the central authority added land in 1953 and 1968 after having acquired it from private owners. And some of the so-called reservations are not juridically recognized reservations at all, that is, land that has been recognized officially by the federal government or the crown. They are *technically* considered squatting zones on which Indians have settled without a formal agreement (Rapport Dorion, 1971: 188–189, 193).

The proprietor of these lands is thus, according to Canadian norms, variable: in some cases, the federal government, in others the province, and in still others the Indians themselves, as is the case of Caughnawaga (near Montreal) where the Mohawks own more than 12,000 acres. According to Canadian law, therefore, most of the Indians of Quebec own no land at all, not even under a guardianship system. They enjoy only a kind of exclusive usufruct that has been granted them by the federal or provincial government in perpetuity at the pleasure of the governmental authorities. The Indians can be moved if a piece of land is found for them, and the federal government may suppress the reservations by law. The Indians are legally nowhere. Even the little land that is recognized as property of the bands is managed under guardianship and cannot be sold without the approval of the federal government. Most of the autochthon residents of Quebec, therefore, have no land at all anymore, either collectively or individually, not even the land on which their own houses stand. The Dorion

Report does not state this so bluntly, but the terms used are very clear (Rapport Dorion, 1971: 209, 213–214).

The authors of the report recognize that it would be unfair to simply abolish the reservations (Rapport Dorion, 1971: 184). They propose that the government should give full ownership of these territories, perhaps after expanding them, to the Indians, collectively or individually, depending on the desire of the applicants. The commission proposes replacing the reservations by communities, where, at least in the first phase, only Indians would reside. Land in the territory of these communities would only be salable by individual Indians with the approval of the band. The Indians would manage and administer these communities, however, in compliance with federal or provincial laws that apply for all citizens. In this way, the commission attempted to convert "the rights" of the Indians into measures that could be implemented in practice (Rapport Dorion, 1971: 402).

A "French" Point of View: The Power of the Written Text

The commission's attempt to trace how the present situation has come about is, it must be admitted, an accurate reconstruction, but the facts are presented in a way that supports Euro-Canadian conceptions of what ought to be done. The authors of the report note the prior actions of politicians, administrations, and courts; they present the precise wording of the *Proclamation royale* of 1763 (Rapport Dorion, 1971: 49), the Indian law, and so on; and they describe what has developed in jurisprudence. They note that most of the Indians were placed abruptly on reservations, without any force being used. The Canadians did not fight; the Indians did not fight; no treaties were signed. By the power of the word, the colonial and the Canadian governments stated and wrote that this was so. And because the French at the time thought and believed that the Indians and Inuit had lost their rights to the land after the colonists had "discovered" this part of the New World and their king had decided that this territory was his, most of the autochthons retained no more land, not even the land on which they lived.

The status of the immense area called the "Indian territory" is less clear. After the capitulation of the French, the British Crown stipulated that these areas could only be taken from the Indians after the Indians' rights were extinguished. Quebec assumed the obligation in this stipulation in 1912, and the matter remains an open question. The Dorion Commission concluded that Indian rights still apply to this territory, even when Euro-Canadian norms are applied. This also applies, they said, though to a lesser extent, to the territory previously granted to the Hudson Bay Company. A glance at a map makes it clear that the Indians and Inuit still have some vaguely defined rights to vast territories. In any event, there remains a kind of usufruct: the Indians have priority for hunting, fishing, and trapping in these territories, and they have the right to live from these activities.

The Dorion Report made no concessions at all to the Indians' position that all previous land acquisitions were only a series of symbolic acts with pen and paper that were never recognized as binding by the autochthons. In fact, written texts did convert huge "Indian territories" into regions where the rights of the autochthons could be "extinguished." This was the case of Rupert's Land, which belonged to the Hudson Bay Company: the king of England, from his throne, "gave" this land to "adventurers," who organized the trade. For the reservations and for the other territories, their acquisition was largely a matter of pen and paper and of traveling to and through the New World. Extensive farming or military occupation after battles and surrender by the defeated parties never happened. The commission, however, did not go into these matters.

Ethnocentric Expertise

The Dorion Report is cleverly written to support Euro-Canadian interests and takes no account of historical interpretations put forward by the Indians and the Inuit. Although the text repeatedly admits that the Indians and the Inuit were treated paternalistically, the report ultimately does the same thing, albeit more subtly. The argumentation in the report is based on the supposition—like the ruling of the Supreme Court that overruled Judge Malouf (Gagnon, 1973: 203–209)—that it is inconceivable, almost ridiculous, and certainly anachronistic to challenge the integrity of the territory of the present Province of Quebec. This integrity is accepted as an acquired right, a historical fact that has been consecrated by the passage of time. The federal and provincial governments ultimately have sovereign authority over all the land that has been depicted in all atlases as "Canada" for as long as anyone can remember. It would be unthinkable, it is suggested, for 30,000 descendants of Indians and Inuit, many of whom are of mixed origin, to reverse the course of history (Rapport Dorion, 1971: 389–397).

The Dorion Report devotes only a few pages (Rapport Dorion, 1971: 339–345) to the position of the Association des Indiens du Québec. In these few pages, it is stated that the demands of the Indians are formulated unclearly; that, for example, "treaties" are cited although no treaties were ever signed in Quebec; that some of the demands are contradictory; and that it is difficult to know what the Indians actually think. In short, it gives the impression that the Indians are promoting obscurities and are poorly informed.

I was myself present—as the only white observer invited by the Indian chiefs—at the meeting of the leaders of the Association des Indiens du Québec held in the fall of 1969 in Sainte-Foy (City of Quebec), and I can testify that the Indians on this occasion presented their demands very, very precisely. That these people from reservations, even though they were assisted by white advisors, were incapable of expressing themselves precisely and in detail in the academic jargon of Western universities is not at all surprising. Canadians from villages or from less well-off or less-privileged social strata could not do so either. But this does not mean that the Indians' reasoning was nonsense or that their demands were groundless. The Indians' demand of 85% of the territory of Quebec as property or an indemnity of 5 billion dollars was not, apparently, taken seriously by the commission (Rapport Dorion, 1971: 8). In its conclusions, the commission proposed a one-time payment of 250,000 Canadian dollars and an annuity of 125,000 Canadian dollars (Rapport Dorion, 1971: 393).

THE PARTI QUÉBECOIS

The "French" as Colonized American Aborigines

Analyzing a number of the basic texts of the present Parti Québecois and its chairman published at the time of our research, documents like *Oui* by René Lévesque (1980), *La nouvelle entente Québec-Canada* (Government of Quebec, 1979), and *La politique québecoise du développement culturel* (1978), one notes an astonishing consistency in the schema that is presented, a schema that runs roughly as follows. Quebec is not like the other provinces of Canada but is rather a homeland of a people with its own culture, its own history, its own language, and its own future. Moreover, its people are one of the two cofounders of Canada, one of the *peuples fondateurs*. For these reasons, Quebec deserves another status than that of an ordinary province.

But there is still another reason: What Quebec actually demands is its *decolonization*. By the victory of the English over the French in the late eighteenth century, the inhabitants of New France were annexed without their being consulted in a system of British colonial construction that was designed to marginalize the French or have them simply disappear by assimilation. At the beginning of this annexation by England, the use of French as an official language was banned for a time. The English backed down on this point in order not to alienate the inhabitants of New France completely at a time when the United States was becoming more and more of a threat.

In fact, the English always kept the French in a subordinate position: first by the unification, and then by means of the federal system. The federal system gives the impression that the French of Quebec were allotted a wide degree of autonomy. In fact, this was never the case. From very early on, the English were in the majority. The demographic superiority of the English was augmented in more recent times by the "Néo-Québecois" (new immigrants, many of whom choose the English side). It assured that many important decisions were in the hands of the English, even when French Power (Monière, 1982) had control on the federal level, for the federal government had ultimate say in all the key economic sectors.

Quebec, in the first phase after the conquest by the English, was passive: the French retreated to a rural economy and lived in relative isolation. This was one of what are called the two *solitudes*. Nevertheless, even in the last century, more than 150 years ago, there were people like Louis Joseph Papineau who did not accept the situation and even led an armed rebellion against the English in an attempt to establish a free state. But Papineau's revolution was overwhelmed, and a severe repression took place. Louis Riel, a métis, also lost his battle and was hanged. The French opted for the preservation of their own culture and their own identity as a people instead of going over to the English, even though there were economic advantages in doing so. The French had little or no capital and virtually no businessmen, but they survived until after the Second World War (Monière, 1982).

Then, people gradually became aware of the technological and economic growth of the outside world, and a *révolution tranquille* took place in these years during which Quebec made up for a large part of its underdevelopment. After the Second World War, the Parti Québecois (PQ) contends, there were demands for more independence and more political power for Quebec, and this took place under all governments and independent of the particular parties in power. There was talk of "equality or independence," "masters in our own home," "cultural autonomy," and the like. At the beginning of the 1980s, the PQ and René Lévesque have talked about *souveraineté-association* (Lévesque, 1980).

According to the *souverainistes*, the Quebecers have always been oppressed: they were first considered by the English to be a conquered people, and later they were forced into the position of a minority, which is increasingly the case today. Population growth, which in recent years has been less among the Quebecers than for the rest of the Canadians, has led to the ever-declining influence of Quebec on important political decisions. "Revenge in the cradle" is obviously a thing of the past. Quebec will thus be further marginalized economically, socially, and culturally, for the other provinces will go along with the federal government when it is in their interest without taking account of Quebec (Monière, 1982).

For all these reasons, said the spokesmen of the PQ, Quebec must cut itself loose from the rest of Canada. French-speaking Quebec must be able to negotiate on an equal basis as an independent nation with the rest of Canada. Quebec must act in its external relations as a perfectly sovereign people and deal with whomever it wishes. Quebec could do this, according to the leadership of the PQ, because it has a territory that is as large as the Netherlands, Belgium, France, Spain, and Portugal combined. Quebec has immense wealth in hydroelectric power and asbestos, and many natural resources have yet to be tapped. Quebec, in addition, can negotiate with the rest of Canada over a new form of economic association so that the economic system could proceed as formerly, albeit with some important advantages for Quebec so that it could be able to conduct an independent economic policy. This, in broad outline, was the core of the political discourse of the PQ and of René Lévesque.

The economic plans for the future proposed by the PQ leadership were based on the "integrity" of the territory of Quebec. Only in passing, however, is there mention of the autochthon population groups. In *La nouvelle entente* (Gouvernement du Canada, 1979), James Bay is explicitly cited, but it is only stated that negotiations have taken place and that, thus, Quebec is lord and master of its territory. As a matter of course, the territory of Quebec is presented as the proper territory, the land of the future nation. The PQ reaches back to the first Frenchmen on the American continent to sketch the origin of the French Quebecers: their forefathers were ambitious men who had penetrated to the Rocky Mountains in the West and to Mexico in the South. They were the first to explore America and certainly the first to occupy Canada. The PQ never mentions colonization of the Amerindians. The French community is not presented as a colonial authority but as a colonized people: the colonists are the English, and the Quebecers of the 1980s are doing nothing other than trying to put an end to this colonial situation. The shame of colonization is shifted entirely to the rest of Canada.

Swallowing the Preaborigines

When one goes back three or four centuries in order to anchor the principle of a people's independence in history, it would seem reasonable to mention the existence of other colonized peoples who lived on the same territory—peoples who had lived there for thousands of years. But the PQ has not done so. The Inuit and the Amerindians have, in the meantime, gone through their own *révolution tranquille* and have objected to the continuation of the colonial situation with at least as much conviction. Today, white "French" are pilloried by the Indians of Quebec as colonizers who are even less trustworthy than the "English." The Amerindians and the Inuit would certainly refuse to make common cause with these other "colonized people," the Quebecers. Moreover, Lévesque and his PQ were seen by many Indian leaders as dangerous opponents, against whom they lost, not in the sixteenth or seventeenth centuries but in the 1970s, an unbloody battle in the form of the James Bay Convention. In the eyes of the Indians, the proponents of independence, the *souverainistes*, were hypocrites who wanted to undo the consequences of English colonization, which had taken place two centuries previously, for their own people, while in the full light of the 1970s they shamelessly continued their own colonization. Precisely the same thing was also being done as regards political independence. The PQ based its demand on the reasoning that a formerly colonized minority with its own history, language, and culture would necessarily disappear if a dominant majority could make the major decisions about its destiny. The Indians, and more specifically the Mohawks, the Attikameks, and the Montagnais said precisely the same thing but were not taken seriously by the government of Quebec.

The *souverainistes* of René Lévesque and the PQ may not be seen as a small group of politicians who were trying to drag along the French-speaking population of Quebec largely by means of manipulation. When the referendum on the independence for Quebec was held in 1980, there were about 8,000 local groups of the PQ in existence, which indicates widespread support. That the PQ came to power twice, even after the failure of the referendum of May 1980, points to the vitality of the movement started by Lévesque in the late 1960s.

The PQ, however, could not claim that it represented all the French-speakers of Quebec who were striving for the continued existence of the French people. Many who belonged to other parties also wanted Quebec to develop politically and economically with more autonomy, although they thought this should be done in the framework of the federal state. They rejected the complete sovereignty of Quebec, even though this would have been tempered by an economic association and a monetary union with a new Canada-without-Quebec.

None of this detracts from the highly doctrinal approach the PQ employed. The official texts, the white papers, the slogans, and the speeches of the leading figures of the party generally adhere to the same rigid reasoning and obviously come from the same limited thought and action circle. At the time of the referendum, for example, the party functioned under strong central control.

Both the PQ and most of the Indians, therefore, demanded far-reaching or total independence. In a certain sense, the Quebecers have less reason for this than do the Amerindians or the Inuit. Nobody denies—indeed the PQ continually cites it—that the French-speaking Quebecers are descendants of a community that was defeated militarily and inhabitants of a territory that was ceded by the "mother country" to the enemy by the Convention of Paris. The PQ has been attempting to turn around this defeat by the English by presenting the Quebecers as war victims who had to yield to the violence of the aggressor. In a time when new military confrontation was unthinkable as an initiative from the English-speaking Canadians and oppression of minorities could only be opposed in the international forum, the *souverainistes* were attempting to escape from two centuries of oppression in a peaceful and legal way. A repetition of the revolt of 1834-1837 and of the repression that followed was unthinkable in the 1970s and 1980s, although bombings by the FLQ and the military intervention in Montreal in 1970 had indeed led to physical confrontation. But the PQ clearly rejected all violence and assumed that it was possible to free Quebec from the surrounding state.

-6-

CLOSER TO REALITY
Conversations with Huron Citizens

When I first came in contact with the Huron Village in 1968, I tried to track down everything that could give indications in any way of the near or distant past of this community. I have since repeated this attempt several times. In 1968, there were four persons in the village who were actively occupied with the history of their nation. Two of them, as far as I know, had no intention of publishing, but the third published a book on the history of the Hurons a few years ago. The fourth amateur historian of the Huron Village returned to his original plan after a few years' interruption and, with the support of the Province of Quebec, formed in 1982 his own team of a number of young people, called the Traditions Huronnes Committee, to trace systematically all the possible historical sources in the Quebec region. This same person was already active in the reconstitution of the history of his people in 1968, though with more limited resources.

THE FEELING OF BEING A DOWNTRODDEN, VANISHING NATION

For dozens of individuals whom I interviewed, it was a fact that they, as a people, were treated very unjustly by the English and primarily by the French and specifically by the Jesuits. In 1968, one year before the publication of the White Paper, I encountered a population, the majority of whom were pessimistic about the continued existence of the Huron community. The French but also "the whites" (the Euro-Canadians) in general were seen by almost everyone as a threat. It was expected that the Canadian authorities would very soon liquidate the last rights (*nos droits*) that still remained to the Hurons, more particularly the right to live on a too-small reservation, the exemption from some taxes, and the benefits from special social programs (social security). The Hurons were afraid that the

"French" would take over their place and that they would cease to exist as a people. This French takeover and the disappearance of the Hurons was seen as the last phase of an inexorable process.

It was generally believed in the Huron Village that the French had taken away land. Which land, precisely, was not so clear for many. Some older people, who have since died, had themselves experienced the expropriation as young people of land that is now situated in the Laurentides Park, north of the Huron Village. And a few others, who knew somewhat more about the history of their nation, would also bring up the Sillery area, which had been swindled from them many years ago by the Jesuits, their legal guardians at the time. Still other lands were mentioned, but the knowledge of them was very hazy for most of the Indians. At the time, I often heard cited the well-known text "as long as the waters flow [etc.], we will respect your rights" (*Tant que l'eau coulera . . .*), which the colonizers were supposed to have said. Although this text had nothing to do with the Hurons historically, it had apparently become common Indian property. Some older Indians alluded, generally in veiled terms, to former chiefs who had severely harmed the interests of their own people by selling large pieces of land on their own authority to outsiders or who had even conspired with the French. Every adult of the Huron Village knows precisely who is meant, but the names are rarely mentioned.

What was known in more detail about "the history" generally concerned the recent or very recent past: what one had heard from one's own father or grandparents; the discrimination one had suffered in school; the working environment, where Indians were laughed at; memories of textbooks and history lessons in which the Indians were presented almost always as a treacherous people and as losers. But some members of the village had a more structured, personal knowledge of the relations between the Hurons and the Euro-Canadians because of considerable personal experience or because they occupied positions of responsibility in the band.

"A," a former grand chief, 80 years old ("his grandfather was true Indian, his grandmother true French"), worked for 25 years as a game warden in Laurentides Park and had also accompanied the whites to Mistassini as an assistant surveyor. "A" considers himself to be a great hunter, and he mourns the decline of the Hurons. "The young people don't care enough about their nationality," he said. "A" holds that one can be an Indian without having the physical characteristics of an Indian. Being an Indian is having an innate nature that cannot be reduced to something else. His father and grandfather were also Indians in this same sense.

The decline of the Indians seems to him to be inevitable: "There is no justice in the world; the strongest dominate." In his opinion, before the young people have learned enough to be able to defend themselves, the Indians will have disappeared, and the English, in particular, are the guilty parties.

The English took over the Laurentides, which was partially the hunting grounds of the Hurons, and made it a national park. They said it was to protect the wild animals. And they did it without consulting the Indians. If the Indians still want to hunt, they have to be careful not to be caught or they are thrown into jail, so they always have to sneak through the woods. The whites do not protect the wild animals at all, for they give hunting licenses for *viande vivante*, to anyone who wants to buy one, even Indians. But the Indians do not want to pay to hunt on what they consider to be their own territory, territory that was taken from them unjustly. Moreover, the whites appoint game wardens who poach and kill game illegally themselves. Further, they do things to wipe out game. For example, they put out strychnine to kill the wolves, but this also kills many other animals. "A" has lived through all of this, and has worked as an official guide for Americans, Belgians, and others.

Another action that greatly harmed the Indians was to place Canadians who had nothing whatever to do with the Indians on the reservation with the same rights as the Indians. The federal government said that this had been done with the agreement of the Indians. The Indians protested later when they saw that the non-Indians began having children and thus posed a threat to the Indians' space. The Indians protested to the federal government, which gave the non-Indians six months to leave the reservation. Most of these non-Indians were married to Indian women and they asked if they and their wives could stay on the reservation while the children would leave. The Indians agreed. But many children of non-Indian origin did not leave. So it is that today there are non-Indians living on the reservation who enjoy the same privileges as the true Indians and who are crowding out the true Indians. They do not belong there. "A" has nothing against the Canadian renters because "you can get rid of them whenever you want."

Indians are also subjugated by the presence and actions of the agent, the representative of the state, if they should act in a way that the state disapproves of. "A" said that he could accomplish nothing as grand chief because he often opposed the agent of the state.

"A" considers it an inalienable right that the Indians have the land "as long as the sun rises, as long as the water flows—but what can I do with a bow and arrow?'' ''A'' argues that infiltration is occurring also in the North, causing the Indians to disappear, and he believes that this will be successful.

''A'' stresses that the ideas and the opinions of the Indians have never been taken into account. A few years ago, a commission went around to investigate the misery and dissatisfaction on all the reservations. They spoke beautiful words and made many promises, for example: ''We owe you more than we ever can pay, but we will do our utmost.'' Nothing came of it. It is always the same: the Indians are simply fooled. The Indians have to be made aware of this. ''A'' thinks that the Association des Indiens du Québec might be able to accomplish something as regards the restitution of the lands, but he is skeptical.

''A,'' a still vital man of 80, gave me the impression of being well-balanced and serene during the two long conversations I had with him. He used no empty slogans and saw the disappearance of his people, whom he had led for a long time, as probably inevitable. Implicitly, his point of view rested on the concept that the authentic Indian life was primarily a life-style, the life-style of the hunter, which presumes that one has land on which one can freely hunt, as was formerly the case. But the Canadians are taking all the land away, and that means the end. My conversations with ''A'' took place in November 1968, before the publication of the Rapport Dorion (1971). He was unmoved by the militant sloganism of some of the young leaders, whom he regarded with some skepticism. If they could accomplish anything, and he hoped that they could, first of all the land should be restored. Having been born in 1888, he certainly had heard much talk about hunting on their ''own land.'' The considerations ''A'' put forward were based on his own experience and had very little in common with politicized discourse or with exaggerated ideology.

THE INDESTRUCTABLE NATURE OF ETHNIC BELONGING

I had the same impression from a conversation, also in 1968, with ''B.'' ''B'' has since died, as has ''A.'' I met ''B'' in the cheap hotel where I was staying (which has since burned and been rebuilt twice) about a hundred meters from the border of the reservation. ''B'' was then 72 years old. When he was young he had left the Huron Village to travel. He presented himself to me as an adventurer. ''B'' had been in the army and had worked on the railway. As a soldier, he had been in England for three years. When he was young, he did not think the Huron Village was worth anything. The acts of the former Chief X, who had sold the lands of his group without the Indians having had anything to say about it, had scandalized him. He also considered the infiltration of the 11 "non-Indians" onto the reservation, and later their descendants, to be very bad. According to "B," the descendants of the non-Indians still had a letter saying that they would be recognized if it were approved by a general vote. "B" contended that this referendum had never taken place. One of the descendants of the infiltrators, who himself could not read, had shown this letter to "B," to which "B" had responded: "If you could read you would never have shown me this letter, for it proves that you have no rights here."

According to "B," who had lived for many years off the reservation, the reservation is a lost cause: "There are no true Indians anymore. Not a single one. Nobody knows the language anymore, and a people that no longer has a language is lost. It will not be long before the Hurons are absorbed." "B" considers "the rights of the Indians" nothing extraordinary anymore: the others (the Canadians) also have health insurance and old-age pensions. "B" is proud that he never profited from his Indian status, "not for one cent." He lives from his military and old-age pensions. Nevertheless, *as an Indian*, "B" feels that he has been offended: the Indians were robbed. When I met him for the second time in 1969, he had moved into a rather dilapidated house on the reservation, where he was living with two mentally retarded sisters and a mentally disturbed brother.

Like the life story of other returned migrants, this interview shows that "B" spontaneously placed his own "Indianness" beyond any doubts, even though he had lived for many years off the reservation and refused to benefit from his Indian rights. That there were no longer any true Indians left on the reservation, in his opinion, did not keep him from feeling cheated *as an Indian*. The indignation manifested in the tone of the conversation appeared to me to be authentic. He minded very much the disappearance of his people, though he considered it inevitable.

THE FEELING OF DYING OUT

As did the conversation with "A," the interview with "B" displayed no conscious cleverness or embellishments. The same realistic tone was also heard in the story of "C" and "D," a married couple, he 80 and she 81, in 1968. Both have since died.

Like "A," "C" experienced the involvement of the Canadian state directly and concretely. "C" was also a hunter, and he could freely hunt in the Laurentides up to a few years after his marriage around 1910. He shot a lot of game, and he sold the hides for fur, necessarily at very low prices, but the hides were easy to sell. Then the state prohibited hunting in the "nature reserve" and appointed game wardens. "C" was caught, fined, and imprisoned.

"C," in his words, was a victim of Chief "X," who sold the land of his own people. "C" lived on the *quarante arpents* (roughly 40 acres) together with his father, two brothers of his father, and two cousins. This land of the band was sold by two chiefs, one of them being Chief "X." Chief "X" was also a relative of "C's" wife, "D," being the brother of her mother. But the families did not speak to each other. Chief "X" had a small factory and provided work for people in the reservation, and he also came to own the paper mill. The people did not dare to vote against him—the ballot was not secret—for fear of losing their jobs. Moreover, Chief "X" could always count on the support of the "non-Indians" of the reservation, for he had promised that they and their descendants could stay on the reservation if they voted for him. The people at the time were still insufficiently educated to be able to protest effectively.

"C" and his family were evicted from their homes. This caused them to lose their poultry breeding operation, their vegetable gardens, and so on. The woods of the *quarante arpents*, which had provided them firewood and building materials, also had to be abandoned. The land was sold at auction and, according to "C," all the families were given five dollars and were promised one dollar per person per year for an unlimited period of time. This one dollar was only paid once. Chief "X" is generally considered a swindler and a parasite.

"C" and "D" were both convinced that things were going from bad to worse on the reservations. The Indians were losing to the non-Indians. One of the non-Indians of the reservation had 18 children, which endangered the rights of the Indians. Within 20 years, the state would say: "On this reservation there are as many or more non-Indians as Indians; you are no longer recognized." "C" and "D" added: "We are two old people; when we die there will again be two less." Neither "C" nor "D" could give much information about the earlier history of the Hurons: neither of them "remembered," for example, much about the former clans or lineages.

Several other elderly people of the village spontaneously expressed the same complaints and concerns. But it was not just the older people who spoke this way. There were also a number of young people who perceived realistically the gradual decline of their people. They placed little faith in slogans or what one of them called *la plume* (the Indian feathers), "the bad myth"—the poorly informed and, in his opinion, dubious slogans—the then grand chief used in TV speeches. All these members of the community were outwardly passive, though as individuals they protested vehemently against the policy of the state and felt that they had been cheated. It is striking that almost all the people of this category belonged to the "political clan" that was then in the opposition. As Hurons, they had the same worries and concerns as their opponents, but they distinguished themselves from their opponents by their opinions on the policies that should be implemented and, more particularly, about the line that had to be used with the general public. They argued for less spectacular and less aggressive language and for a serious, historically supported presentation of their cause. They did not appreciate the "show" that their leader put on.

Thus, there is continuity with the past, despite everything. People admit that there are non-Indians among their ancestors and that the future is dark. Yes, frauds were perpetrated not only by "whites" but also by their own leaders. But none of this implies any threat for their own identity as Indians, *true* Indians. Some older people hunted on their own collective land, and this distinguished them as Indians from Canadians. They also knew a time when there were at least a few people on the reservation who knew the Huron language. The theme of the infiltration of the non-Indians, who politically belong to the opposing faction, is vivid for all of them. They distinguish themselves as Indians clearly from these "non-Indians." The young people who consider themselves to be of this category identify with these old people as with forefathers who still lived in the tradition.

MODERN TOOLS FOR TRADITIONAL SURVIVAL

In 1968, the mood of many who belonged definitely to the party in power was much more optimistic. They had more hope in the continued existence of the Hurons as a people, although some of them were uncertain about the ultimate outcome. It is striking that the members of this "political clan" employed a harder, more sloganistic language, were openly engaged in ideological construction, and backed spectacular actions. Most of these people knew very little about "the old days" and were linked to the outside world in one way or another through commerce or a small business. They stressed the oppression of the Indians by the "French" and the "English" in general. They were silent about the "non-Indians" on the reservation, who, in any event, belonged to their informal political grouping.

"E" has a shoe factory. He is enthusiastic about the political activity and the policy of the grand chief. With the current grand chief, the village is vital. "E" employs about 20 people in the Huron Village. He wants to expand his business and build on a new industrial park that is planned for the near future. "E" sells shoes throughout Canada and says that his clients like to buy Indian-made products because Indian work is better. When I pointed to the machines with which his "handmade" shoes are made, "E" defended himself in nationalistic terms: "We have adopted a few techniques from the whites, but they have taken our land, our language, and everything from us. . . . The province [the provincial government] is a swine and the federal [government] is rotten!"

"E" is convinced that the Huron Village will continue to exist on the basis of the "treaty," despite the fact that no "treaty" was ever signed with the Hurons. The children will also remain Huron: "It's in their bones." "Their favorite game is to dance Indian dances dressed like Indians."

"F" was 26 years old in 1968, was single, and operated a tavern and store. From his family tradition, he belongs to the opposition, but he himself has joined the other side. The impression "F" gives is primarily that of a merchant. He complains that the other Indians on the reservation do not patronize his store: they do almost all their shopping off the reservation. They buy from him only when they are in need, when they have debts. The Indians will not buy from him because of jealousy: they do not want one to become richer than another. The Indians want everybody to be equal. "F" can get no money to expand his business: as an Indian, he is considered a minor and his creditors cannot take him to court. Therefore, they are not prepared to advance him very much.

According to "F," all Indians are agreed that they want to remain Indians. He would like his children, when he has them, to realize that they are of Indian descent. According to "F," the young people are not influenced by their parents in the choice of a marriage partner. A marriage with a Canadian is not considered less desirable.

Two years previously, the Indians had blocked the road through their reservation (a rather important arterial) in order to dramatize their demands. According to "F," the grand chief who organized this demonstration is a good defender of Indian rights—better than his predecessor, who was a good man but poorly educated, and so on. For the last few years the reservation has been developing, and there has been progress. Nevertheless, "F" feared that the reservation will be assimilated and saw this to be inevitable.

"F" knows very little about the past. The question of the *quarante arpents* means nothing to him. He knows that there are two political factions on the reservation, and they make a great deal of fuss at the elections. He thinks that these groups were always there but he does not know how they started. He does not seem to know anything at all about the existence of the "French" or the "non-Indians" on the reservation.

"G," with a helper, makes canoes, which he sells in his store. He is middle-aged. "G" does not think that the reservation will disappear: the children of some Indians who had left the village are returning. They have married outsiders because they had to: too many people on the reservation are much too closely related. Many Indians only left because they wanted to earn money.

"G" thinks that the grand chief was doing very well. He considers the relationship between the Indians and the "Canadians" (the "non-Indians") on the reservation of no importance: everybody is mixed with everybody anyway. "G" disagrees with the idea that he should be considered a Canadian and says that nobody in the village wants to be so considered. This belonging to the Indian nation is transmitted to the children. The parents, according to "G," do not want their children to marry non-Indians. For 50 years, he says, the state has been trying to wipe the Hurons off the map. But "G" is not pessimistic about the outcome. He thinks that the Hurons will continue to exist. And "G" considers it normal that there are two political groups in the village: that is the case everywhere. In his opinion, it did not arise because of any abnormal conflicts.

Although it is impossible to divide up the entire population of the Huron Village, person by person, into two political categories on the basis of interviews, occasional conversations, and participant observation, everyone obviously recognizes that there are two parties that primarily manifest themselves every two years, at election time, when the band council is elected. Insofar as these two groups were visible to me in 1968 and 1969, they can be characterized as follows. In principle, a person belonged to group 1 or group 2 by descent, although one could change from one to the other. Normally, it was expected that each would follow his or her family tradition. Formerly, the voting took place by a show of hands, and so voting behavior could be observed. Now the vote is taken in secret. Since these two groups have been about numerically equal over the last 20 years and thus have maintained themselves in equal proportions, one may assume that there were few shifts from one group to the other.

Group 2, in recent years, seems to have opted for "development": the grand chief, who had been in power since 1964, was himself a merchant and a small industrialist and had taken a considerable number of initiatives to make possible the creation and development of other businesses on the territory of his reservation. A relatively important expansion of the reservation territory occurred in 1968 with the addition of a piece of land on which small factories could be built and expanded and dozens of new houses built. A local "bank" was founded to help Indian businessmen with loans. Looking back today over the last 20 years, one sees that an economic development occurred under the government of this same grand chief that marked a new era and that had already begun to surface in 1968-1969.

It is striking that the category of merchants and small businessmen I have cited here, and who depend for their business on the outside world of Canada, used a harsher political language than the members of group 1 and also were much more aggressive in the public forum. "H," the grand chief, often spoke on radio and TV and at public occasions in the 1960s as a "harsh" political speaker. What "H" told me in 1979, in a Quebec hotel where everybody seemed to know him, does seem to be true: "I oppose the Canadians very strongly, but they respect me." As a businessman and as a private person, this leader is, moreover, a friendly and engaging man who could influence his clientele positively and even win them over. The new merchants and businessmen approve of his external policy. The combination of political and commercial success makes "H" vulnerable to his opponents, who accuse him of using the political forum to promote his business.

"H" became the leader of the Hurons in 1966, and he was still in office in 1982. I had several conversations with him in 1968. He formally gave me permission to carry out my research on the reservation and, ever since our first meeting, continued to be friendly and supportive. "H" was then secretary of the Association des Indiens du Québec and member of the administration of the National Indian Brotherhood.

"H" was convinced that objective research could only benefit the case of his people because in this way international attention would be called to the grave problems of the Indians in Canada and, more particularly, in Quebec. According to "H," nobody knew the Indians: "The Canadians do not want to study the matter seriously; they do not want us, period." "H" stressed that the Hurons had almost disappeared a few years earlier. People had become indifferent. "H" regretted that the complicated and difficult Huron language was no longer known, except for a few words. He held the Jesuits responsible for this, as they had forbidden the Hurons to speak their own language. The Jesuits are also to blame, "H" maintained, for the loss of the land: when they arrived in Canada they only had the cross and the Bible. Now the situation is just reversed. Being a practicing Catholic did not keep "H" from maintaining that the subjugation of his people occurred through the agency of the Catholic church.

According to "H," a few years before (around 1964), some people of the reservation became aware that, culturally and ethnically, they were dying out. "H" then looked around for ways of refinding his roots. In June and July of each year, he invited Indians from other, more isolated reservations to a powwow. At these celebrations, Indian dances were held along with typically Indian contests, such as the portage race for canoes. Most of the Indians invited to the powwow still had their own language and culture. These contacts made the Hurons aware of how much they had lost, even their own language. "We were almost totally Canadianized. By this contact a new awareness was created and it has been intensifying."

"H" stressed that the Hurons had become more individualistic than the Indians of the North who have remained traditional. "In my home, for example, each child has its own room. The father no longer knows what is going on in his house. This is not the case in the North, where everyone lives together in one room." Further, there are more and more marriages to Canadians.

"H" also stressed that many industries have developed on the territory of his reservation, and he personally gave me a guided tour of the most important factories. In his own factory, for example, 27,000 pairs of snowshoes were made in 1967 by a crew of five people. Most of these craftsmen were related to him.

The Indians of Quebec did not have the right to vote in provincial elections in 1968. They were dependent on the federal government. The minister, a Canadian, does precisely what he wants to do with the proposals submitted by the Indians. The Indians want an Indian for minister, but the Canadians refused to permit this.

From the first private conversations I had with "H," there emerged a picture that closely approaches reality, as I was able to determine by further research. There was no pompous political ideology dished out, nor was there any pretense that the Hurons had preserved a typically Indian culture. On the contrary, "H" himself spontaneously emphasized the state of far-reaching disintegration of the cultural integrity of his people. The content of these conversations contrasted sharply with many passages of the book *Le premier des Hurons* (Gros-Louis, 1981), which I discussed above. The discourse developed in this book comes very near the style and ideology that "H" uses in his public appearances. I will return to this question.

Outsiders who are not familiar with life on the reservation could receive the impression that only the grand chief and his immediate supporters seriously wanted to be and remain Indians, while the mass of the reservation population could more readily be assimilated. Nothing is less true. The "silent majority" is attached to the past at least as firmly as the ethnic leaders. One could even say that group 1, historiographically considered, is more authentic, more solid, because its members develop virtually no idle slogans and associate themselves in a more direct and visible way with the Huron past.

INDIAN TRAITS AND ETHNIC FEELINGS: CULTURE AND ETHNICITY

In summary, the opinions in the Huron Village in 1968 on the survival chances of the Hurons as a people were divided, but everyone agreed that the Hurons had been badly treated in the past. No one wanted the Huron group, as such, to disappear. Even the "adventurer" emigrant, who had been away from the reservation since his youth, felt strongly that he had been deprived of his rights as an Indian. The view most people had of their own situation and of their relationships with the dominant majority of Canada was realistic. In the life within the village, almost all of the adult population stood far removed from the simplifying and manipulative ideologies that would be developed in the 1970s by many Indian leaders in their public writings and speeches.

In 1968, when I studied the Hurons, I had already completed fieldwork among the Yaka of Zaire, a people who had remained very traditional. I was skeptical about the "Indianness" of the Hurons, and I sought without success for weak points in the desire of this people to survive. In the dozens of interviews and informal conversations, I was unable to detect any weak spot at all in the presentation of the Hurons as a "we," as an ethnic group. The loss of many of their own customs and of their language was regretted but calmly admitted, and seemed to take nothing away from the strength of the ethnic-front formation.

THE CULTURAL FOUNDATION OF HURON ETHNICITY

I wondered then whether other cultural elements might be hidden in the community of the Huron Village which were not explicitly cited in the conversations but which still gave the group its own coherence. Perhaps there were cultural elements that were so much a part of everyday life that one was not clearly conscious of them.

The first fact which emerged only indirectly in 1968, seemed to be the unambiguous geographic localization of the Huron community, its *spatial identity*. In several interviews, references were made to "the Canadians," "the non-Indians," "the French." "I," a middle-aged man who was a shoemaker, told me that he found it unfortunate that the Hurons were forced to buy land to build new houses while there was reservation territory occupied by "the Canadians." This reference to Canadians can only be understood in a metaphorical sense, for he probably knew very well that hundreds of Canadian renters were living on the reservation in rented accommodations with the full consent of the Hurons. He was not against these people, but rather against the much fewer number of "Canadians" who let themselves pass for Indians. As in the interviews cited above, the territory of the village, as a residential area, had a symbolic value: it is an Indian reservation that possessed the innate nature and tradition of the group. One could settle there as a stranger, provided one had permission. But whoever entered as an autochthon without being an autochthon or gaining permission committed an offense against the nature of the community. The reservation was a piece of space that was even recognized by the dominant majority, officially, as belonging to the Hurons. It symbolized the integrity of the group, just as a "fatherland" does for many nations. The territory of the reservation was felt to be the last piece of land that remained to the Hurons. All the rest had already been taken away. And in this sense, the reservation was an irreplaceable *cultural element* of the group.

The reservation is also an element in the system of concrete human relationships, both synchronically and diachronically. Whoever lived there with full rights, as a co-owner, was a Huron and not a Canadian. Therefore, "the Canadians" should not be permitted to live there. The ancestors of the Hurons were established in this place and had lived there for more than 300 years. All the Hurons of the last centuries were born on this land; the dead are buried there. This reservation is a place that marks a person.

The massive reaction against the 1969 White Paper, which advocated that all reservations disappear within five years as *specifically Indian spaces*, indicates that the situation is at least analogous on many other reservations. This same theme also emerged in the discussions regarding the granting of the right to residence and of other rights to non-Indians married to Indian women and to the children born of these marriages. In this context, too, the fear was for a "Canadianization" of the environment. This continuity with the past, maintained by owning and living on demarcated territory, has nothing to do in my opinion with ghetto formation.

Another sector of the ordinary, daily life that for years has given a continuity to the cultural uniqueness of the group is the manufacture and sale of handicraft objects. Everyone in the Huron Village knows people who make mocassins, other leather articles, snowshoes, and canoes. The continuity in this area is well documented, although there has been a major change in the techniques of manufacture and in the style of the objects. (Mechanization, for example, has affected style.) The maker of snowshoes by hand must ask about five times more than that charged for the same machine-made article, which makes the handmade product virtually unsellable. Craft articles have thus not remained independent of modern technology or of the market economy. But the very fact that objects are produced that are analogous in style, function, and material to what was formerly produced creates a continuity that distinguishes the inhabitants of the Huron Village from the surrounding Canadians.

That dozens of Hurons are active in the handicraft sector is an objectified form of continuity with the past, a kind of culture production and reproduction of which the content is less important than the activity itself in the understanding of the continuity with the past. The Indians have a sort of moral monopoly on this kind of handicraft product.

If one examines the objects produced and analyzes them in terms of art history, one may conclude that no object for sale in a local store has anything to do with the products of the Hurons of the pre-Columbian period and even little to do with the culture of the Hurons of the nineteenth century. The canoes are no longer made of bark and are no longer repaired with resin; the leather jackets with fringes have nothing to do with the former clothing of the Hurons, nor do the headdresses with feathers down the back. Most of the mocassins are at least partially machine-made and not from the same kind of leather as previously; miniature objects, like the small tomahawks and most of the beadwork, are fodder for tourists who want to buy cowboy-film stereotypes for their children or relatives. Nevertheless, any French Canadian who would produce such objects would be branded a forger.

Moreover, the legal recognition by the state of a person as an Indian living on the Lorette reservation (thus, the sanctioned biological continuity) is another powerful factor that contributes not only to ethnic but also *cultural* uniqueness. Whoever is recognized as a Huron will also bear, so it is assumed, culture-specific traits that may not be immediately apparent but that can manifest themselves in the form of life nuances and self-esteem. This specific sense of self-esteem, which may or may not be difficult to define from the outside, thus becomes itself a cultural element.

Thus, there *are* cultural elements that make the Huron community a group with its own character, notwithstanding the acculturation and assimilation that has occurred in many areas of life. The Hurons need no inflated "Indian" ideology, based on incorrect facts, generalizations, and "pan-Indianism," to establish their continuity as an ethnic group. The discourse that some Huron leaders developed in the 1960s and 1970s was, in my opinion, generated by a political situation in which the dominant majority postulated a specific, stereotypical picture of "the Indian" that included a number of clearly perceivable characterizing emblems: Indians do not dress like Canadians; they look different, physically; they live in teepees or in another type of construction that differs substantially from that of the housing of the Euro-Canadians; they live by hunting, trapping, and fishing; they speak their own, incomprehensible language and live "in group." During my appointment as guest professor at the Université Laval in Quebec in 1968, I heard often the spontaneous comment that the Hurons were actually no longer Indians. Even in 1982, some of my Canadian colleagues in other fields expressed surprise that I, as an anthropologist, would be occupied with the Hurons of Lorette.

The leaders of the Hurons who appeared in public in the late 1960s had little choice of the means they could use to legitimate the existence of their community as a specific group. They had to meet the pattern of expectations of the Euro-Canadians and the wider world public, at least to a certain degree. Thus, they provided emblems that were considered absurd by many Indians of the reservation. I frequently heard comments like this: "We can be Indians just as well without all these things."

Leader "H" and his brother wore their hair in 1968 differently than the rest of the residents of the village: a long braid over the shoulder and short in front. This short hair was intended to recall the *hure* (French for "bristly hair"), from which the French colonizers were supposed to have derived the name "Huron." The Hurons were formerly called the "Wendat." In reality, the hair style of the pre-Columbian Wendat was much different from what "H" thought, and it is probable that this etymology of the term "Huron" is a popular interpretation. *Huron* also means in French a "rustic rural resident," so the name "Huron" need not have anything to do with the word *hure*. Leader "H" had also replaced his tie with a beaded medallion and sometimes wore mocassins instead of shoes. The wearing of these "traditional" emblems, however, never caught on on the reservation: everybody continued to dress inconspicuously "Canadian."

Some traditional symbols had more success, however. A number of Indians of the Huron Village added Indian names to their French-sounding ones in the 1970s. New, wooden street signs were made in an artisanal fashion, and new bilingual (French and Indian) names were invented, reflecting passages of Huron history. Totem poles and some teepees were exhibited on the reservation. Of all these emblems, the Indian names may have proved in the most convincing way that not just the leaders but also the other Huron citizens meant what they said.

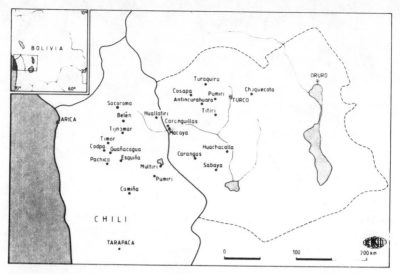

THE AYMARA OF TURCO
Hurons in Reverse

TURCO IN BOLIVIA

Another member of our team, G. Pauwels, conducted five years of fieldwork (beginning in 1975) among the Aymara Indians of the Altiplano of Bolivia, specifically in the village of Turco. Pauwels reconstructed how the Aymara, over the course of five centuries, evolved in identifying themselves ethnically. He also analyzed the involvement of the Aymara, in the period 1975–1980, in the broader social context of Bolivia. I draw on Pauwels's work (*Dorpen en gemeenschappen in de Andes*, 1983) to discuss the case of an Indian group that has retained large amounts of territory under collective ownership. They have also preserved their language and a number of their own cultural traits and institutions. During the colonial period, the Aymara were exploited by the Spaniards, largely as conscript labor for the silver mines. A small number of Spaniards settled in the midst of the Aymara and treated them as inferior *Indios*. At the end of the colonial period, by a rather complex interplay of factors, the Spaniards were largely absorbed by the Aymara.

In 1975–1980, the interethnic oppositions between Aymara and Spaniards had receded completely into the background in Turco. They have been replaced by territorially defined groups and a situation in which social identity is expressed in terms of clear socioeconomic differences. This has been fostered by the national government, which grants economic and social benefits to *regions* and *localities* rather than to ethnic groups. In recent years, the people of Turco have been attuned to "progress" and "economic development," and they define themselves in the way most apt to extract benefits from the government.

The Aymara of Turco live very far from the urban agglomerations and have only limited knowledge of the Euro-American culture of the dominant majority. Nonetheless, they know what economic development means, and they expect only positive things from it: more wealth, more status, more prestige, more comfort, and more social security. At the time of the fieldwork, they accepted "civilization" with little reserve.

Still, their ethnic identity survives in the background. In 1975–1980, the Aymara now and then demonstratively presented themselves to the outside world as Indios—for example, when one or another agency or international organization indicated its willingness to finance a development project for the benefit of the "poor Indian population" for which the Aymara consider themselves eligible. Whereas the Hurons of Quebec, with whom this book is primarily concerned, are building ethnicity almost from historical scratch, the Aymara reject their ethnic tradition, although they use it in an instrumental way when it pays off. A comparison between these two groups seems promising.

The discussion of the Indians of Quebec showed that the rise of ethnic self-affirmation under the banner of "own culture," "the right to remain different," "own tradition," and "being an independent people," is related to a broader political context that rewards such self-affirmation in one way or another. Under the conditions that prevail in contemporary Canada, ethnic self-affirmation may not only provide self-affirmation and feelings of pride—the sense of being someone irreplaceable—but can also be an effective way to increase one's material resources beyond what could be expected from competition in the labor market. Thus, ethnicity can be a matter of being but, at the same time, it can also be a matter of "getting" and having as well. Paradoxically, being traditional can be helpful in acquiring more modern goods—with the accompanying lifestyle that demolishes tradition.

These main conclusions drawn from the Hurons are confirmed, almost in reverse, by the Aymara case. As we will see, in 1975–1980, the period of the Leuven research, the Aymara of Turco consciously dropped and destroyed their customs and traditions in an organized, active, and self-critical way. They energetically expunged what the Hurons, at the same moment, tried to reconstitute. Quite reasonably, in their own eyes, they hid their ethnicity as much as possible, identifying instead as members of a socioeconomic class or stratum. In other words, the Aymara tried to disappear as bearers of a particular cultural tradition. Their main fear was that they would not succeed in doing so: that they would not be able to overcome their dualistic cultural and religious belonging, and that the dominant majority would refuse to allow them to "pass" because of the Aymara's phenotypical characteristics, their language, and their Indian way of life. The Aymara try to make themselves invisible in the same domains of social life in which the leaders of the Hurons try to make themselves as visible as possible.

Nevertheless, as we shall see, the same human dynamics are at work here, and the same theoretical framework used in analyzing the Canadian material will resolve this paradox.

FIGHTING TRADITION AND ETHNICITY FROM THE INSIDE

The Aymara of Turco live at an elevation of 3,700 meters on the Bolivian Altiplano. The population density of this region is less than one inhabitant per square kilometer. In the colonial past, the inhabitants of Turco belonged to a "free" region, although they were exploited as forced labor in mines, and the Turqueños still kept large areas of land that they held in collective ownership. There are even a number of descendants of whites who had themselves registered as Indios in order to be able to own land outside the village.

Even though Saints Peter and Paul did not found Turco, as the local tradition has it, the village is still an institution that was imposed by the colonists. The Indian groups were previously grouped in ayllu or communities that remind one of ethnic groups. The ayllu was a widespread type of autochthonous community in the Andes. It probably developed out of a territorial kinship group into a form of territorial unit. The ayllu had a regime of common-ground property. The colonists on the other hand built nucleated villages, and the important people of the colonial system, such as the pastor and the judge, lived in them. Gradually, the village replaced the local community. This structure imposed from without also altered the Aymara culture and society. And although many Aymara were known for their stubborn aloofness and their rejection of any trappings of Western civilization, even in the present century, those of Turco resolutely have opted for the way of "civilization" in the last few decades. They have even interiorized their "inferior" position. In recent years, they have held weekly and sometimes more frequent village meetings to discuss how they best could promote the further "progress" of their village and how they might win themselves recognition as an important urban center in the near future in order to become the capital of a new and independent province. For the realization of their plans, the residents of Turco are completely dependent on the central government. The central government, which is controlled by the dominant, non-Indian, socioeconomic groups of the country, strives to split the Indios into local entities and to use them against each other. In the period of the Leuven research, subsidies and development projects were not awarded to ethnic groups or peoples but to administrative zones and localities. For the residents, it was, therefore, pointless to present or identify themselves as Aymara, for this was not only irrelevant but even undesirable in the eyes of those who distributed the resources.

In the cities of Bolivia, however, Indian movements started to form from the 1970s and even earlier. These movements are launched and led by descendants of Indians who are highly acculturated and who are in intense contact with non-Indians. The Aymara of Turco, however, live in a very rural area and remain removed from these movements, partially because of their lack of formal education. They have been abandoning their traditional customs rapidly, chasing what they call "modernity" and "progress." The Turqueños are a textbook example of subjugated people who come to believe in their own inferiority, and who consider the absolute superiority of the subjugators as invincible truth.

SUPERIOR MODERNITY

An old Turco man, one of the most respected figures in the community, tells the following story:

> We are all born from one and the same mother. The color of our skin is different, but we are all born from one mother. The eldest son was a *negro*. The one in the middle was a *trigueño*. This is the color we have, the *Indios*, as they call us. And the youngest was a *blanco*. These are the Spaniards. The white boy was more appreciated than the black one and the *trigueño*. The youngest one was the most beloved and the smartest. He was the worthiest. The *trigueño* and the black did not mean much. And that's the way it still is today. I have been able to witness it myself. The youngest was very bright, but the other ones did not progress. The eldest and the second respected the youngest. He was reflecting about everything and moved ahead in all matters. These are the Spaniards and the other ones who live there. The *trigueños* are fools and bums. The youngest is capable and intelligent. This is still the same in our families: the youngest is always the most talented. The oldest is always slightly stupid, and so is the middle one. They are not worth very much. The youngest is always the most skillful and the most ingenious. That's what people say. (Pauwels, 1983: 46)

For the storyteller, the inferiority of the Indians and the superiority of the whites are givens from creation that cannot be changed much. In the meantime, most of the residents go as far as they can along the way of the whites. The only thing that makes them feel inhibited is their appearance, their phenotype, which prevents them from being whites.

The Aymara of Turco do not call themselves Aymara or even Indio, except in confidential, private conversation. These two terms have too many overtones of the "savage" and the "retarded," of the underdeveloped and the nonevolved.

They identify themselves instead as residents of Turco, Turqueños. By using this geographic name, they avoid references that are, they feel, less favorable. They even do this when they speak of their origins. They attribute the foundation of their village, and thus of their group, to the settlement in their village by Saints Peter and Paul. According to Turqueños, these saints arrived with the Spanish conquerors. Turqueños assume that people were already there at the time of the conquest, but not much is said about them. In any case, in the late 1970s, the residents of Turco were of mixed genetic and cultural origin, and about half of them had been Christianized.

THE FUTILITY OF BEING A NATIVE

The Aymara lack the context of the Hurons for presenting themselves as an ethnic group. Their reference group has, since the independence of Bolivia, consisted of the higher social layer of the *vecinos* ("notables") (Pauwels, 1983: 178). The vecinos were originally whites who moved into the village after the mines closed and when the law permitted them to live in the villages of the Indios. Very soon, sexual relations between these whites and the local women produced mestizos, who shared the status of their parents (Pauwels, 1983: 184). This category of people married with the traditional leading families of Indian *caciques*. The caciques in this way formed the bridge between the whites and the mass of Indios and mestizos.

The vecinos remained an exploiting group, even after decolonization (Pauwels, 1983: 217). They were the only ones who could read and write; they became local judges and took advantage of the people in administrative matters. They also executed the wills of those Indians who had written them, and in this way obtained lands that had been the collective possession of the Indios. Many notables registered as Indios (*communarios contribuentes*) (Pauwels, 1983: 224) in order to participate in collective land ownership;

at the same time, they continued to act as members of a higher class in the village and in the region. The Indios rebelled violently against these exploiters in many places and at various times in the province (Pauwels, 1983: 243–245).

PASSING

Gradually, the Indios were acculturated through contact with the *residentes*. These were emigrant Indios who kept a house in their village and maintained ties there. The emigrants defended the interests of their village in the outside world. Indios in the village grew more open to the model of "civilization" and "progress" represented by the notables of the village. Particularly since 1952, a spectacular movement has developed away from the *costumbres* (the traditions and customs), away from what clearly distinguished the Indios from the others (Pauwels, 1983: 335). Many communarios listed themselves officially as mestizos although they were "biologically" not mestizos (Pauwels, 1983: 352). They had themselves registered as monolingual Spanish speakers, although they either spoke Aymara in their daily activities or, at least, knew it perfectly well. A comparison between censuses conducted in 1942 and in 1975 is shown in Table 7.1.

Personal names were adapted to Spanish. The patron saint and the church or chapel built to his or her honor became the primary means of group identity for many residents of the region, and (as elsewhere in Latin America) fiestas were held yearly in honor of the patron saint by communities. But in 1975–1980, even this custom was thrust into the background. The residents of Turco even sold 50 kilograms of silver that belonged to the church in order to invest in the development of the village (Pauwels, 1983: 365).

Until the early 1980s, the residents of Turco appeared to be doing everything possible to forget their ethnic identity. They understood that they were perceived by the outside world as Aymara and Indios—as backward— but they tried to overcome this backwardness. This meant equaling as quickly as possible the knowledge, the abilities, and the achievements of the whites.

HOLY TEMPTATION: THE WORLD OF CATHOLIC GOODS

The residents of Turco have little or no understanding of national, let alone international, relations. They are unaware of the effective use of

TABLE 7.1

The Self-Identification of the Population of Turco (1942–1975)

	"Race"		Language		
	Indigéna	Mestizo	Aymara	Aymara–Spanish	Spanish
1942–1945	87	13	87	13	0
1946–1950	97	3	78	21	1
1951–1955	94	6	71	22	7
1956–1960	77	23	54	30	16
1961–1965	23	77	26	55	19
1966–1970	40	60	5	10	85
1971–1975	60	40	6	2	92

NOTE: Figures are percentages.
SOURCE: Adapted from Pauwels (1983: 335).

ethnicity by groups like the Huron, for example. The idea that a formerly colonized people could assert itself by emphasizing its cultural and historical uniqueness and presenting itself as a nation seems inconceivable in Turco.

Instead, the majority of Turqueños have a negative self-image of their Indianness and are involved in "two worlds": the world of the devil or of the Inca and the world of God or Christ and of the Spanish or civilization (Pauwels, 1983: 111). Their spontaneous remarks at unguarded moments show that the conflict between these two worlds has not yet been definitively settled. The world of the devil, of pre-Columbian Indian culture, still lives in them to a degree, and thus they are not yet completely what they should be. Turqueños must break away from the world of the devil by orienting themselves completely to civilization. They have internalized the negative image that the Spanish missionaries and colonists drummed into them. The superior material products of the whites were and are a confirmation that whites are better. Even the religion of the whites is superior, for "the forty nations" (the whites) received their technology from their god. Like the members of the Cargo Cults in New Guinea (Schwartz, 1976), Turqueños perceive material culture as an emanation of the religious.

Few external factors promote transcending this negative self-image. On the contrary, the term Indio remains synonymous with backwardness, lack of education, and a rustic life-style. The government defines the campesinos (peasants) as a poor portion of the population that must be helped with its problems and its development, and the term campesino has no ethnicity component. Help, resources, and development assistance are given to localities and not to ethnic groups. Important areas defined as urban centers or sections of a province, receive the most help, so it is materially advantageous for a community to become recognized as such a center as soon as possible. Turqueños speak wistfully of becoming city dwellers—at least in their own little city if they cannot actually migrate.

For most Turqueños, the concepts of development and progress are not based on knowledge of the outside world but are idealized. In contrast with the Hurons, the people of Turco have no daily contact with the dominant majority that lives in the city. They no longer have any local opponents. The whites and mestizos who lived among them have left or have been absorbed into their ranks (Pauwels, 1983: 231). There are still vecinos, but these people are no longer whites or mestizos but promoted communarios. The previous ethnic oppositions have been replaced by socioeconomic oppositions. At one time in the 1970s, one could register as a vecino. One joined this category by accomplishments and by being recognized as such by others, not by being born into it.

In South America, it is the most urbanized Indios who start Indian nationalism movements. Rural people who have virtually no contact with other ethnic groups can hardly imagine that affirmation of an ethnicity—one that has always been stigmatized as inferior—could possibly be advantageous socially or financially. The international trend toward ethnic self-affirmation has not penetrated to the Aymara of Turco.

THE "SAVAGES" OF THE AYMARA: ETHNICITY IN THE PAST

Throughout the last four centuries, however, we also see in this part of the world, the Altiplano of Bolivia, processes that are similar to those occurring in Quebec and on other continents. Even before the conquest in the sixteenth century, there were, in the region surrounding modern Turco, groups of peoples called savages by the Caranga, the ancestors of those who are now called the Aymara (Pauwels, 1983: 141). These peoples, the Qhoru or Uru, themselves formed distinct communities with various names. They lived primarily on water on reed floats, and subsisted by fishing, gathering, and hunting. According to present-day Aymara traditions, they were already in the world when only the moon shone before the sun existed. When the Uru heard that the sun would soon rise for the first time, they expected it from the West and so oriented the openings for their huts to the East. But the sun rose in the East and burned most of the Uru, who could find no protection from its heat in their huts. A few escaped by jumping into the water from which they emerged later on and multiplied (Pauwels, 1983: 62–63).

It has been demonstrated historically that the Inca took at least some of these "savages" from the water and put them on the land. But the Inca also seem to have treated them as an inferior group. During the Spanish colonial period, the Uru were considered so impecunious that their taxes were minimal and they were virtually exempt from forced labor (*mita*) in the mines.

Today, there is only one group of Uru remaining in the Turco region: the Chipaya. The other Uru have disappeared, probably mostly by "Aymarization." The Uru presented themselves as Aymara only when the tax pressure and the forced labor were eliminated (Pauwels, 1983: 272). In this way, they participated in the ownership of land without being exploited as the Aymara were. They also escaped the stigma of being "savages," constantly driven (by the Aymara) off the land allocated to them and back to the banks of the lakes and rivers.

Only the Chipaya have preserved their "own" language, clothing styles, and housing against the surrounding Aymara. But the culture of the Chipaya actually is composed of elements adopted earlier from the Spaniards and the Aymara—elements that now have disappeared from these groups. The Chipaya have had to defend themselves against the surrounding Aymara and have succeeded by discovering irrigation. They dug a five-kilometer canal, allowing them to grow crops and to raise pigs and goats; they have even become specialists in making goat cheese. Moreover, the Chipaya have recently discovered that they, as a small group that has preserved its "traditions," generate admiration from the outside world and, as such, can obtain financial and political support rather easily, whereas the acculturated Aymara cannot.

Among the Aymara there is still the feeling that the struggle between the Inca and Christ is not yet over. It is *possible* that the Aymara will eventually join the growing Indian movements, since they feel that they do not yet completely belong to the Kingdom of God. But there remains among them a tension between ethnic pride and self-depreciation. They express a feeling of continuity with their ancestors and with their past, even while they talk about "progress" and about not being Indios.

"UNETHNIC" CONTINUITIES WITH THE PAST

Considered from the standpoint of observable culture, the Aymara are embraced in a double religious system that was constructed in a complex way. First, they identify themselves with the Christian saints who distinguish their respective communities within the village and their village from other villages. The fiestas and the *cargo* system (the burdens that each person in turn has to take to organize and give feasts at his own expense) are a complex of activities that were imposed by the Spaniards. (Through this cultural complex, the Indios were simultaneously exploited and made and kept Christians [Pauwels, 1983: 460–463]. In recent years, the system has changed or collapsed altogether, and Turqueños now say that they were slaves of the local priests because of the cargos.) On the other hand, close examination reveals that in and behind the Catholic rites are celebrations related to components of "traditional" religion such as Pachamama (Mother Earth), the spirits of the hills, what local people call "the devil." Until recently, blood sacrifices (*wilancha*) were made.

Everywhere there is evidence that the pre-Christian religion is interwoven with Catholic tradition. Thus, the leaders in traditional religious matters, the *yatiri*, are said to be appointed by "Santiago," Saint James, and it is also said that the yatiri can survive Santiago's lightning (Pauwels, 1983: 516–518). And the crucified Christ, on Holy Thursday, is not associated with Christianity but with the devil because he was crowned king by the "evil people" (Pauwels, 1983: 513).

The situation is even more complex, for in 1975–1980 there were new Christians and old Christians. To the European missionaries who succeeded local priests in recent times, the Catholic feasts appeared pagan. The missionaries tried to impose restrictions, particularly regarding the consumption of alcohol, and have largely eliminated the cargo obligations, which were under their authority. The Catholics, in the light of the new Catholic catechesis and of the teachings of the Gospels, had themselves become pagans of a sort to more recent missionaries, and now there are, alongside the *católicos, catequistas* or new Catholics in the village, people who follow the teaching of the missionaries and who have abandoned the old "superstitions." The new church communities have undermined belief in both Pachamama and in the *santos* (Pauwels, 1983: 523), and the people of Turco have come to accept that there are three *sectas*. It is no longer demanded, as used to be the case, that evangelical converts who, for reasons of principle, rejected the cargo system, leave the district. This attitude of pluralism marks those Turqueños who have turned resolutely to "progress."

THE AYMARA AND THE HURONS: THE UNIFYING POWER OF PRACTICAL REASON

The process of ethnic synthesis and change now taking place among the Aymara is, at bottom, the same as that among the Hurons. From the sixteenth century on, two dominant factors determined relationships between ethnic groups: the need for material survival and the desire to improve material living conditions, social position, and relative status associated with improved material conditions. When they have a socioeconomic interest in doing so, the Uru become Aymara; as long as this is not the case, they remain Uru. The Aymara never allowed themselves to be completely incorporated by the Spanish colonists. The Aymara accepted the Catholic religion, after a fashion, but did not abandon their own culture entirely. As long as they felt threatened as a people, they remained faithful to their native, indigenous spiritual forces: their ancestors, the spirits of the hills, and Mother Earth. They reinterpreted most of the elements of Christianity in terms of their local religion and magic. With the reforms of the 1950s and thereafter, the Aymara observed that they could advance socioeconomically by moving to the cities and by urbanizing their own village. They quickly yielded their attachment to their own costumbres, orienting themselves totally to what they refer to as progress. The socioeconomic advance of the communarios was facilitated by schooling and the subsidizing of local projects by the government, and by the fact that many of the vecinos, the Aymara's neighbors, who were predominantly mestizos, had emigrated to the city or were absorbed by the Indios.

By the same token, many whites and mestizos who belonged to the *vecindario* (the rural elite) had themselves registered as communarios contribuentes (members of the Aymara community per se) in order to take advantage of the collective land ownership of the Indios. Whites and mestizos needed this land to raise pack animals and produce animal fodder. These people, too, played both sides; they kept their own ethnic identity—an identity that permitted them to exploit and dominate the communarios in other sectors of life. They had the power to enforce this double identity, and did so.

This process was driven by technical know-how. The Spaniards, of course, maintained from the sixteenth century on that they brought civilization to the New World, and this involved, along with Catholicism, a particular life-style and a certain technology. Indians had reason to associate the superior technology with the imported religion—a religion which had conquered the paganism of the devil and of the Inca. As elsewhere in the world, nobody had to convince the Aymara or the Hurons of the superiority of Western technology: the Indians observed this themselves and set out to acquire the products of this technology. At the same time, both the Hurons and the Aymara have found it useful in recent times to flaunt their native culture to powerful people in the dominant urban areas of their respective domains. They act this way because it pays them to do so, and it pays because at least *some* members of the dominant elite are sensitive to and have sympathy for the "old peoples"—for Indians—who have remained themselves and who still have authentic, "natural" cultural products.

This part of South America is also trying to achieve "white" attainments. Of course, one could say that the Aymara and their ancestors have been strongly indoctrinated for centuries: their view of themselves as children of the Inca who also became children of the victorious *santos* is evidence of this. Higher social status and higher human and religious ways of life have always been associated with the social categories and groups that dominated the Aymara and that, in spite of everything, became their reference groups. But this is only a part of the explanation.

The Aymara see more opportunities for a better life in urbanization and social promotion in comparison with the old-fashioned villages and towns: "The others will look up to us." So it would seem that the Aymara, like the Hurons, search for and find values in "modern civilization" that they do not find in their own system.

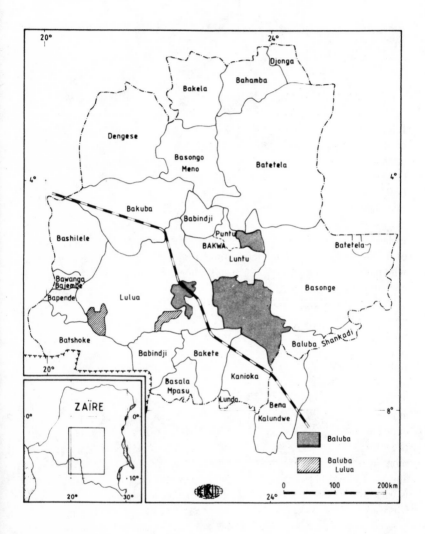

20°

24°

Djonga

Bakela   Bahamba

Dengese

Basongo
Meno   Batetela

4°   4°

Bakuba

Babindji

Bashilele   Puntu

BAKWA   Batetela

Luntu

Bawanga
Bajembe

Bapende   Lulua   Basonge

Batshoke

Baluba Shankadi

Babindji   Bakete

20°

Basala
Mpasu   Kanioka

Lunda   Bena   8°

Kalundwe

Baluba

Baluba
Lulua

ZAÏRE

0°   0°

0   100   200km

10°

20°   30°   24°

-8-

THE LUBA OF KASAI (ZAIRE)
New "White" Ethnics

PREETHNIC "NATIVES"

It has often been taken for granted that the ethnic group belongs to primitive or at least ancient history. Patterson, in his book *Ethnic Chauvinism* (1978), strongly favors that position. However, 15 years ago, Campbell and LeVine (1974) had already shown that the tribe or the ethnic group is often the creation of missionaries, at least in black Africa, or it is a form of organization that comes about in rather complex societies.

I came to the same conclusion in my fieldwork (1961–1965) with the isolated and "traditional" Yaka of Zaire: the "Yaka people" had nothing of a seamless tribe, but were constituted of a delicate layering of groups who partially melded together. The way ethnic belonging was manipulated came quite close to what I would later observe with the Hurons of Canada.

The Luba and the Luluwa are an extreme case: they became ethnic groups only in the 1950s, following a strong development in the direction of the modernizing Western culture. Their violent conflict, in which thousands of people died, had nothing to do with an upsurge of "primitive," "tribal" fights. Ethnicity can be old, or quite young. Rather, it is timeless, or of all times.

The study *L'ethnogénèse luba* (1985) by Mukendi wa Meta, a researcher at our center, focuses on two groups of people who gradually came to be called the Luba and the Luluwa. Both groups had common ancestors in precolonial times and, although they distinguished themselves from each other by clan membership, they all called themselves Luba. Today, the Luba and the Luluwa both claim to be descended from *Sangu Lubangu*, which is variously a tree, a territory, or a lake situated somewhere in the present Kasai or in Shaba region (Mukendi, 1985: 58–59).

According to Mukendi, the predecessors of the modern Luba and Luluwa saw themselves as related to each other, either through marriages of the children of their leaders or by political lord–vassal relationships. One thing is certain: when the first white people appeared in the region, the Luba and the Luluwa were not two ethnic groups in opposition to each other (Mukendi, 1985: 69–70) as they are today. Just before the arrival of the whites, the Luba were intensely harassed by the Tshokwe, who had introduced slavery and firearms into the region. A number of Luba found shelter from the Tshokwe with the ancestors of the present-day Luluwa, which has led some authors to suppose that the Luba were slaves of a kind. According to Mukendi, one must rather speak of a patron–client relationship. The relationships seem to have been good, and many marriages took place between the two categories of people, both of whom called themselves, at that time, Luba.

Ethnic (rather than political or social) differentiation between these populations became conspicuous with the arrival of the colonizing Belgians. Many predecessors of the present-day Luba were indeed partly nomadic in this time. They readily established relationships with the misssionaries at the mission stations. They converted to Christianity, and were cooperative and enterprising. Many Luba attended the schools of the missionaries and soon took jobs in the colonial administration. Others became skilled laborers.

The demand for Luba laborers was particularly high during World War II, when great efforts were needed for the production of rubber and other products. In time, tens of thousands of Luba spread out over the entire territory of the colony. Very often they occupied the most advanced positions. Their attitude toward, and ability to adapt to, the colonial system contrasted sharply with that of, for example, the Kuba, a proud and dominant neighboring people who had long refused to collaborate with the whites. The predecessors of the present-day Luluwa also participated in the colonial system to a lesser degree than the Luba from Kasai (Mukendi, 1985: 105 ff.).

Gradually, the Luba or Luba-Kasai, came to form throughout the Congo a socioeconomic class that was the closest to the whites: under the Luba, there were many *évolués*, people who were capable of living like white people, who frequently owned their own homes and lived in the better "native" neighborhoods. In the cities, the Luba distinguished themselves from most of the other native groups by their education and lifestyle as well as by their phenotype, at least according to the popular view, for the Luba have a strikingly lighter skin color than most other Zairois. By 1959, as the Congo was to become independent, the Luba-Kasai formed a visible social class, both in the region of Kasai and in the city of Luluabourg, where they lived together with the Luluwa, and in the surrounding area.

THE HISTORICAL GROWTH OF ETHNICITY

These events did not, by themselves, produce ethnic conflicts in the urban centers of the Congo or in the Kasai region. Even in the late 1950s, the Luba–Kasai were not a well-organized ethnic group, though the Luba who had moved to the cities had formed local associations where they could meet and reinforce their ethnic identity. At the time, however, their ethnicity implied membership in a socioeconomic stratum and, while ethnicity and socioeconomic status may have been mutually reinforcing, they also obscured each other.

Municipal elections were organized in the Congo in the late 1950s, and the candidates who had identified themselves as Luluwa defeated the Luba. This was the first event that marked strong ethnic consciousness among the Luba of Luluabourg. The Luba candidates had identified themselves primarily with their respective clans, and each went their own way without worrying about the Luluwa competition. After the elections, they presented themselves much more strongly as a unified ethnic group and formed a political party that gave their ethnicity form, namely the Mouvement Solidaire Muluba (MSM) (Mukendi, 1985: 149).

The Luba in Kasai, as everywhere else in the Congo, strove for independence for their country in the late 1950s. The Luba occupied, certainly in Kasai, the best and most desirable administrative posts and considered themselves the most suited to succeed the whites in positions of power. The Luluwa were threatened by this expression of superiority on the part of the Luba and wanted a gradual transition to independence. In any case, before independence was granted the Luluwa wanted to have things straightened out in what they considered their own region of the country (Mukendi, 1985: 149). The Luluwa demanded that "undesirable" Luba—those who were not merchants or who did not fulfill a function that was useful for the native Luluwa population—leave the Luluwa territory within two months. This was to take place after the white administration appointed a traditional chief of Luluwa origin as king of the region. The candidate whom the Luluwa put forward as king, Kalamba, would become the legal owner of all the land, even that on which the Luba lived (Mukendi, 1985: 150). Recognition of this plan by the white colonial government would actually have been a total creation, for there had never been such a thing as a king in the Luluwa region. This was, in fact, collusion between the Luluwa and colonial administrators, for the whites tended to support the Luluwa, who wanted gradual independence, rather than the Luba, who wanted independence (and power) as soon as possible. In an official report (the Duquenne Report), the colonial government supported the request to recognize a Luluwa king (Mukendi, 1985: 150–152). The royal pretender, Kalamba, inspired a Luluwa resolution, published on June 20, 1959, demanding that Luluwa authority over the land be recognized by everyone and that the Luba who failed to do so be expelled.

On August 3, 1959, the colonial administration arrested Albert Kalonji and other Luba leaders who had attracted a large following among their people. On that occasion, too, about a thousand Luba people were sent back to their region of origin, in the rural areas of Kasai. The press agency Belga spoke of the arrest of troublemakers (Mukendi, 1985: 153). On October 11 of the same year, riots broke out between the Luluwa and the Luba after Luba youths had insulted the Luluwa of the Union Congolaise party and Luluwa women had reacted by dancing naked on the street (*kujibuila*), which symbolized a cursing of relatives (here the Luba). Hundreds of Luba were killed (Mukendi, 1985: 154).

At a conference in Matamba in August 1959, 115 traditional Luluwa chiefs decided that the Luba had to leave their territory before September 15. For their part, the Luba chiefs met in Tshibata at the urging of the Mouvement Solidaire Muluba. They prepared for a possible exodus and decided that all Luba, wherever they might come from or whoever they might be, would be welcome anywhere in Luba territory; clan membership would be ignored. This meeting in Tshibata crystallized Luba ethnic unity (Mukendi, 1985: 156–157).

Further discussions between the Luba and the Luluwa did not lead to an agreement: the Luluwa held to their position that they were the owners of the land and that the Luba had not complied with Luluwa customary law and so had to leave. The Luba tried to defend a "modern" interpretation of land tenure, but without success. The situation was very dangerous for the Luba. There were approximately 75,000 Luba in the midst of 600,000 Luluwa in the Luluabourg district. Arson, slaughter, and plunder against the Luba broke out, and an exodus of Luba started moving in the direction of Bakwanga under inhuman conditions. The colonial authorities were not able to maintain order (Mukendi, 1985: 170–172).

In the provincial elections of May 1960, just before independence, Patrice Lumumba, the future prime minister, supported the Luluwa, who voted for the Union Nationale Congolaise, a party associated with the Mouvement National Lumumba. Albert Kalonji and his party, the Mouvement National Congolais Kalonji, won 21 of the 70 parliamentary seats, the most of any party, but he was not involved in a serious way in the formation of a provincial government. He demanded from the colonial government that a separate, independent province be formed for the Luba-Kasai. When he did not get this, he proclaimed on August 8, 1960, a month after the independence of his country, an independent state, the Etat Minier, with Bakwanga as the capital (Mukendi, 1985: 176–179).

The prime minister, Patrice Lumumba, who already had had to cope with the secession of Katanga Province, sent troops to Kasai, and they plundered, stole, raped, and murdered. The armed resistance of the people was answered with still more violence. Between 5,000 and 10,000 people were killed among the civilian population. Finally, President Kasa-Vubu deposed Lumumba and recalled the army (Mukendi, 1985: 179–181).

In the meantime, the Kasai Coalition, under the leadership of Grégoire Kamanga, emerged to demand the territory that was bounded in the north by the basin of the Sankuru, in the east by Sankuru and the Bushimai, in the south by the provincial border, and in the west by a line that ran from Tshikapa to the mouth of the Loange. The indigenous population of this region would have comprised the Kete, the Lele, the Putu, the Bena Nkamba, the Sala-Pasu, the Lualua, and the Bindi. These groups, who considered themselves the first residents of the region, refused to recognize the legality of the conquest of their lands by "Mupemba" (the Luluwa) and by the "Muluba" (the Luba) (Mukendi, 1985: 168–169). These groups were prepared to grant them usufruct rights to these lands. But their demands were without result.

On March 31, 1961, Albert Kalonji appointed himself *mulopwe* on his own initiative. He requested this appointment from a group of traditional chiefs whom he had called together for a meal in his village. The traditional authorities were surprised by the request of Kalonji, their host, and seem to have gone along with the request in a vague sort of way. In fact, the traditional investiture of a mulopwe follows a ritual schema with official personages who invest the candidate with his power. The one who receives power must also inherit it from members of his family in the male line. Kalonji had not respected these conditions and rituals (Mukendi, 1985: 201–205).

The repercussions of this theatrical gesture, by which Kalonji gave the impression of returning to a Luunda kingdom, were enormous. With this gesture, Kalonji reached the high point of his popularity among the masses. By becoming mulopwe, he became the mediator between the ancestors and his people and also the highest traditional political authority, ruling with a kind of divine right.

Kalonji had assistance from two chambers: the Legislative Assembly (composed of members chosen directly by the population with universal suffrage) and the Traditional Consultative Council, which was formed by the traditional chiefs. The latter appeared to be submissive. Gradually, Kalonji began to act like an absolute monarch. He flagrantly favored his family members and friends, had people arrested on dubious grounds, and disdained the rules of democracy. This made him more and more enemies, particularly among the educated and the political leaders, more and more of whom left the region and protested in Kinshasa about Kalonji's administration. Finally, Kalonji was deposed (Mukendi, 1985: 205 ff.). In the meantime, his actions aroused strong ethnic consciousness among the Luba of Kasai, a consciousness that would persist.

In 1982, more than 20 years later, Mukendi studied stereotypes in two groups of university students who came from different regions and ethnic groups. He found that the self-image and the image that others had of the Luba reflected the image that was held on the eve of and immediately after independence. The local radio in the region of the Luba–Kasai begins its programs with *Kasai wa batoke* (Kasai of the whites). One also hears: *Kasai wa balengele* (Kasai of the best). The Luba are called "the whites of Zaire." In Mukendi's study, the Luba were described by themselves and by others as intelligent and enterprising, and far more so than other groups. They see themselves as inventive, creative, idealistic, seekers, scholars, organizers, politicians, all-knowing, persevering, hard working, clever, athletic, productive, dynamic, and rich. Physically, they consider themselves attractive, not only because of their light skin, but also because they are taller than the other ethnic groups (Mukendi, 1985: 224-228).

The subjects of Mukendi's study, taken from different ethnic groups, appeared to use a kind of ethnic scale: on one end are the Luba, who approach the whites by their intelligence, their education, and their working ability; on the other side are the Tetela, about whom it is said that they practiced cannibalism up until recently, a practice considered as belonging to the primitive past. According to Mukendi, it is clear that the young Zairois students who participated in his study apply an evolutionary perspective as a matter of course; primitives are at the bottom and the "evolved" and Westernized are at the top (Mukendi, 1985: 228-229).

THEORETICAL REFLECTIONS

The Luluwa majority leaders reached back to a nonexistent tradition when they decided to have a kind of "king" appointed. Centralized, monarchical power is not part of genuine Luluwa tradition and runs counter to the relationships from the precolonial time, but it draws the line between Luluwa and Luba. The Luluwa purposefully added elements to their tradition, and they found the support of colonial authorities *in the very contestation* of the colonial, "modern" interpretation of land possession that was introduced by the authorities themselves. Similar to the Quebecers, the Luluwa, who talk about *their* territory, are rejected by a number of other local people as the landowners. The "authentic" natives demand the land for themselves and reject illegal occupation by others. Like the Indians before the 1960s, however, the "authentic," pre-Luluwa natives lacked the power and the resources to have their claims heard.

The conflict over land between the Luba and the Luluwa forced the development of conscious, militant, and belligerent ethnic groups. That both the Luluwa and the Luba succeeded in mobilizing feelings and actions by appealing to "tradition"—the "enthronement" of Kalonji is a good case in point—demonstrates that the feelings of the masses are not troubled with historical accuracy. On the other hand, note the similarity in the critical reaction by some Amerindian leaders to the "unauthentic" claims of the Hurons in the question of the Quebec Territories, where the "fake" Huron demands were perceived as jeopardizing the genuine rights of the other Indian groups. The opponents of Kalonji were the "intellectuals" and "modern" politicians who felt disenfranchised by the mulopwe and who objected to the lack of authenticity of the enthronement.

In the precolonial era, the Luba were migrants who came to settle among the Luluwa, and there was no conflict between these two populations in the Luluabourg region. In fact, one can hardly speak of ethnic distinctions between these populations until the Luba, by their association with the whites, advanced socially and economically. Tensions were generated to the degree that the Luba favored their "own sort" within the modern sectors where they were in charge, as in school, the lower administrative levels, and the service sector. But these tensions did not produce open conflict. When it became clear to both parties, however, that one group would dominate the other after independence, direct confrontation and tragedy resulted. Some refer to the process as "retribalization." But this is a misnomer because the process has nothing to do with a return to a precolonial past when Luba and Luluwa would have related to each other like "tribes," which they never did. The ethnogenesis of the Luba–Kasai is a process indicative of modernization and urbanization, and with the socioeconomic competition and status hierarchy that comes with a Western model of civilized society. The forces on which the leaders of the respective groups call are, in a certain sense, timeless: admit solidarity with relatives and with those who have given life (the ancestors) and give these bonds precedence over relations with outsiders; act in accordance with these feelings and be legitimated in the defense of one's "rights" and in the knowledge that one is certainly not inferior to "the others."

Precisely as in the case of the Hurons of Quebec, all the parties involved try to obtain an advantage that enhances their instrumental capacity: one wants just as much and, preferably, more resources than one's opponent— more land, more political power, more socioeconomic promotion, education, and so on. One of the ways to obtain this objective is to appeal to tradition, even when this involves a thoroughgoing reinterpretation of the past. The result of the process is people who want to acquire and develop "new," "modern" cultural elements while still remaining faithful to "tradition" and in this way to distinguish themselves from others, who are doing the same thing and who compete with them for material resources, a constantly recurring pattern in each of the situations we have considered.

Furthermore, at the observational level, peoples become more and more alike and strive for uniformity, even while they try to differentiate themselves in certain culturally expressive domains of life. By this differentiation, people define themselves individually but also try to gain instrumental advantages. And in this way, the sharp opposition between Western culture with its highly developed scientific and technical sectors and the more rural, preindustrial life-style is, in a certain sense, bridged: the traditional peoples demand their independence and modernize themselves at the same time without losing face. Thus, the expressive and the symbolic, in the sense of the not-directly-instrumental, receive new importance and a new status in the present. Moreover, all the parties involved may use concepts such as "culture," "cultural uniqueness," "past," and "descent" in a confusing way, so that very many aspects of what happens are obscured.

The prima facie impression given by movements and actions that focus on ethnic or cultural elements is that such movements are about a return to the past. For ethnicity explicitly appeals to the idealized past. Expressions of loyalty to one's *own* family and people refer inevitably to common origins and thus the past. The popular Western idea of primitive communities is a caricature. It has "primitives" living in "tribes" that are in a constant state of war with each other. This stereotype is reinforced when Westerners hear native leaders talk about the past in the same breath as infranational or micronational self-definition and militancy against rival ethnic groups. Family, past, descent, community and solidarity of people, traditions, and cultural uniqueness stand in the current Western cultural pattern in opposition to individualism, privacy, cosmopolitanism, international interests, and openness to becoming acquainted with and understanding other cultures. Thus emerges the strong impression, even among some scholars (Patterson, 1978), that native peoples are going through a reversion to, and are irresponsibly taking refuge in, a past that is forever gone and that can offer no solutions to present problems. In fact, modern ethnic orientation involves a return to a past that is often not even a "half-truth," a past that has been arbitrarily reconstituted and that serves a group of people as they try to go forward at the same time. The cases in which groups of people—not individuals or communities formed voluntarily—demand simply to return to "earlier" conditions and persist in this demand are, as far as I know, quite exceptional.

The ethnic orientation of the groups I have studied up to the present, considered in terms of this interpretation, is, *among other things*, a covert retreat from the dominance of the former colonizer or from the dominant group or groups involved. This observation is not an ethical value judgment. But the ethicist will, like myself, have to place such a covert retreat in a "history of battles" where the story generally begins with an admittedly enterprising but oppressive Westerner. The tentative conclusions I have drawn here on population groups from developing countries apply equally to ethnic minorities in modern, industrialized Belgian society. This will become clear in the following chapter.

-9-

ETHNIC MINORITIES IN BELGIUM
Among Potential Equals

Islamic immigrants in Belgium comprise a case in which ethnic identity is kept alive or created in a modern, urban setting. They also illustrate some of the complications involved in organizing a multicultural society even in nation–states where all the parties involved, both the majority and minority populations, agree on the right of people to maintain their identity as a matter of principle. In addition, at least one aspect of an important historical event is highlighted: the making of Europe at the grassroots.

BELGIUM: A MULTIETHNIC SOCIETY, WHETHER IT WANTS TO BE OR NOT

Belgium is often depicted in the scholarly literature as a modern state that has to cope with an endemic case of antagonism between two ethnic communities, the Flemings and the Walloons. The small German-speaking population of Belgium is rarely mentioned, and not many outsiders know that approximately 1 inhabitant in 11 is an immigrant from southern Europe, from Turkey, or from other countries. At present, hundreds of thousands of migrant workers, their wives and children reside in Belgium (Dumon and Michiels, 1987; official figures 1984: 270,521 Italians, 55,952 Spaniards, 70,033 Turks, and 119,083 Moroccans; total population: 10 million). Most of the first-generation immigrants claim that they will return to their country of origin, and so, they say, it is only logical that they do little or nothing to adapt to the surrounding Belgian majority. But, as the years pass, many remain in Belgium with their families, and show no signs of imminent departure. Very few ever request naturalization or actually change their nationality (Dumon, 1985: 54; Rosiers-Leonard and Polain, 1980:

128   *CREATING ETHNICITY*

70–71), although some immigrant organizations demand for immigrants the right to vote (Anciaux, 1978: 48 ff.). Although the government classifies immigrants officially as aliens, who, it is assumed, will leave the country one day, their children are sent to Dutch- or French-language schools where little or no notice is taken of the culture and language of the countries to which the "alien" children should return. And all of this occurs in a country where all relations between the two local groups, the Dutch-speaking Flemings and the French-speaking Walloons, are regulated in every detail to assure equal access to all resources. Before going further into the life of the immigrant populations, I will discuss briefly the interethnic relations in Belgium. For it seems to me that the way in which the two native majority groups in Belgium relate to each other has created a semiconscious perceptual framework that assigns a specific place to each immigrant from the outset.

NATIVE COMMUNITIES:
ETHNIC SPLITTING AS A FASHIONABLE TREND

A False Picture of the Ethnic Past

Several influential scholars have pointed out in recent publications that the common notion about Belgium—that it is a state created by a forced marriage between two peoples who have always lived in opposition—is incorrect (Lijphart, 1981; Roosens, 1985). The two large communities, the Flemings and the Walloons, indeed, were not always structured as they are today. When Belgium was founded in 1830, the everyday language of the educated class was French, even in Flanders, where the language of the masses was Flemish, a variant of Dutch. The enmity of both the North and the South was at that time directed against a common oppressor, King William I of the Netherlands. The present-day opposition between Flemings and Walloons has developed gradually since then. Early in the nation's history, a small group of Flemings argued that an injustice was being committed against the people by the imposition of French in the political, judicial, military, cultural, and administrative sectors. By sheer demographic expansion and institutional democratization, the Flemings gradually succeeded in getting Flemish recognized as a national language and in having language use specified geographically in the country. Language and descent became congruent for both sides in their respective territories (Huyse, 1981).

Ethnogenesis: A Process Growing over the Years

This process of ethnogenesis proceeded smoothly on the Flemish side because the Flemings could, with their own language, set themselves off against a native French-speaking population. The language of the Walloons was used in national-level institutions and the French-speaking group leaned strongly toward the cultural world of France. Compared with the Flemish variety, Walloon nationalism is a more recent phenomenon. The term "Wallonia" came into use only after 1850. Until recently, most politicians responsible for the southern portion of the country spoke of Wallonia as an economic region, the viability of which they had to defend, rather than as a region inhabited by a people with its own culture. Flemings, by contrast, created a national consciousness by appealing to the emotional and symbolic importance of language use ("The language is the entire people"), by actively enhancing their own cultural traditions, and by renewing cultural identification. Only later did Flemings begin to speak of Flanders more explicitly in economic terms. Today, relations between the two groups are defined by territory, language, culture, and descent, as well as by economic competition. All these factors have come to symbolize one another in the political discourse of both camps as well as in the mass media.

These years of explicit association of language, territory, relative status, and ethnic identity with political and economic rights automatically impose a special status on people who enter Belgium as immigrants: they are "aliens." Alongside being-Walloon and being-Flemish, Belgians widely recognize that being-alien entitles people to a number of rights and creates for them certain duties under a kind of natural law. But few Belgians are prepared to see Belgium as a country where, together with the Flemings, the Walloons, and a small German-speaking community, other groups of people with their own cultural traditions can settle and remain settled.

"Strangers": A Clear-Cut Category

Many Belgians expect the "aliens," especially those who come from non-EEC countries such as Morocco and Turkey, to return to their country of origin or to make themselves invisible by cultural assimilation and naturalization. For Belgians, the customs, values, and institutions of the "aliens" remain alien. Those customs do not belong in Belgium as permanent realities: Flemings belong in Flanders; Spanish in Spain; Italians in Italy;

and so on. There is also a hierarchy of ethnic groups; some are more "alien" than others. But none are felt to be of equal value with native Belgian cultural traditions. This hierarchy is reinforced by and reflected in the prevailing economic relations between native Belgians and the alien guest-workers.

A Recent Distinction: EEC-Strangers and the Others

Since 1985, however, new currents and patterns of thought have developed. The EEC countries have agreed that by 1992 Europe should become united—with no frontiers, tolls, tariff barriers, or discrimination between the citizens of the different member states. This idea has been launched and repeated over and over again in the media. The far-reaching decision for unification by the EEC governments is based on the idea that the countries of Europe cannot otherwise compete successfully with Japan and the other Asian countries as well as with the United States.

In order to contribute to this growing unity in Europe, a major exchange program, the Erasmus Project, was devised to allow about 10% of all students in higher education to spend at least one semester in another European country, the home university giving credit for the courses attended abroad. This exchange program also includes university professors who are visiting one another's institutes of higher education.

Although no studies have yet been made on the subject, there is a general feeling among those in charge of migrant questions and social services that an increasing number of Belgian natives are prepared to accept the presence of other Europeans on their soil as an inevitable outcome of the historical developments now in progress. This posture, however, does not apply to immigrants from non-EEC countries—immigrants such as the many Turks and Moroccans who today work in Belgian factories—despite the fact that the EEC authorities recommend acceptance and incorporation of these immigrants. Political recommendations are one thing, social acceptance is quite another, and it is clear that nationalistic feelings are far from dead, no matter what the EEC governments decree. A major event in the banking sector in 1988 led to visible and public antagonism between European nations on the Belgian scene. An Italian industrialist, Carlo De Benedetti, tried to take over one of the most venerable and powerful institutions in Belgium, the Société Générale de Belgique, which owns some 25% of all Belgian companies. Nationalistic feelings emerged quickly and strongly. A number of Belgian political figures used every legal means to delay or stop the takeover, arguing that it would be counter to the national interest to allow it to go forward.

Local businessmen put up a financial fight and tried to buy out the raider. A battle developed between Belgian, Italian, and French businessmen. The topic became all-important on television news and in the newspapers for weeks in a row, a kind of international soap opera. American weeklies reported on the matter. Flemish–Belgian television reporters even traveled to Italy to interview "ordinary people" in local, open-air markets. These Italians, many of whom counted migrants to Belgium among their own family or among their friends, were excited by the prospect that an Italian businessman was going to "buy" Belgium with his Italian money. Obviously, among Italian working people, these feelings had nothing to do with personal profit but everything to do with national pride. They saw an inversion of power relations between the rich Belgians and the poor Italians in this form of Italian raiding of Belgian business firms. One middle-aged Italian interviewee told a reporter that it would be a good thing for Belgium to be in the hands of a big Italian boss.

Within the Belgian camp, native ethnic opposition emerged, or at least came to the foreground. The major Belgian antagonist, a prominent businessman of Flemish origin, made it quite clear that if he managed to keep the Société Générale out of foreign hands a significant number of positions on the board of directors would be given to Flemings. It is widely known that the upper management of the Société is a bulwark of Francophones. The saving of the besieged Belgian–Francophone empire would thus become recognized as a Flemish deed.

These public events, documented in excruciating detail and commented on by the media, clearly show that nationalistic and ethnic feelings have not vanished, not even in the most educationally and politically sophisticated circles of the country.

Transcendental feelings for the larger whole of Europe were totally absent in this financial battle. The Italian businessman tried to play the European card, stressing repeatedly that he was merely doing what so many other leaders were preaching, namely, establishing a truly *European* company that would be strong enough to compete and survive on the world level. This European argument was not taken seriously by anybody, either in Belgium or in Italy.

The need to unify Europe, though openly professed by almost every political leader, does not even prevent the Belgian native communities from open conflict. In 1987–1988, Belgium had a government crisis lasting for more than five months due to "linguistic conflicts" in a rural village. How much more difficult will it be to eliminate conflict between native Belgians and immigrant populations?

THE FIRST GENERATION: "NATURAL" ETHNICS

A Useful Underclass

The hundreds of thousands of guest-workers who now reside in Belgium did not come at one time. As early as the 1930s, the coal mines in particular recruited foreign labor to make up for shortages on the local labor market. After World War II, this recruitment accelerated, even though there were then about 100,000 unemployed Belgians, who apparently considered working in the mines too dangerous and too ill paid (Aerts and Martens, 1978: 12–47).

In 1945, with the approval of the government, recruitment campaigns were organized for the Walloon and Limburg mines, and, in a short time, more than 60,000 workers were hired, most of them Italians. It is important to stress that these workers did not come to Belgium on their own initiative. They came at the invitation of Belgian employers to fill jobs that Belgians did not want. By working in the labor-intensive coal industry, the immigrants contributed to the supply of cheap energy, which certainly benefited Belgian competitiveness. Given these clear economic advantages to both sides, neither the government nor the labor unions opposed the continued importation of foreign labor. Moreover, the foreigners were no threat to Belgian workers, since immigrant laborers were permitted to work only in the coal sector for a limited number of years. As it became apparent that this labor strategy was successful, the steel, construction, service, and other sectors in the 1960s requested permission from the government to import workers. Jobs that Belgians would not do were taken by the foreigners.

The importation of cheap labor also saved many employers the expense of costly capital investments. This seems to have been the reason that demand for foreign labor continued even during times of economic recession. After 1967, when the first immigration freeze was announced (a more stringent freeze followed in 1974), a market for illegal foreign workers developed. Their number has been estimated at 20,000. In the meantime, work permits continued to be issued to spouses and children of workers who had immigrated legally.

Experts agree that the guest-workers have become essential to the Belgian economy. Today, the immigrants are an important part of Belgian demographic reality, both because of their labor and because they are consumers as well. This was particularly true for Wallonia in the 1960s, and it will remain so in the coming years (Dumon, 1985: 56; Martens, 1973: 235).

During the early years of the guest-worker migrations, there are few references in documents and publications to the problem that injustice of cultural differences might cause in Belgium. Immigrants were just cheap labor, suitable for the less attractive jobs, and that was that. When the labor pool in southern Europe began to dry up in the course of time—one critical event was a mine disaster in which a large number of Italian miners were killed—the recruitment shifted further to the south to deep in the High Atlas.

Wherever they came from, as soon as they arrived in Belgium the immigrants became part of what Rex and Tomlinson (1979) call an "underclass." Employers could attract workers from southern Europe, North Africa, and Turkey because economic conditions in those areas were so poor and because the socioeconomic class from which employers recruited was so vulnerable. Even before they arrived in Belgium, the immigrants were ranked low on the Belgian social scale. International relations between North and South ensured that from the start. The low social status of immigrants in Belgium is thus not solely a Belgian product, but the dominant Belgian majority confirmed the status differential immediately. No one has ever been prepared to import workers who would compete with Belgians on an equal basis.

"Nouveaux Riches" in the Home Country

Nevertheless, it seems to me somewhat one-sided to consider the foreign workers only as victims of a capitalistic system. Most of the immigrants see their employment in Belgium as an opportunity for economic advancement that is not available in their home region. Members of our University of Leuven team who have conducted detailed fieldwork in Sicily and Morocco, and also other researchers, point out that migration to industrialized Europe is looked on favorably in those countries, and migrants gain socially and economically in their home regions (Heinemeijer et al., 1977; Leman, 1982). Migrants visit their homes on vacation and reinforce the prestige of "guest labor" by bringing many relatively expensive "modern" presents for their family members. The migrants demonstrate their wealth by the fine cloth, the electronics, and the automobiles they bring back with them.

A man might employ a dozen people in the local construction sector in Morocco under the supervision of a brother while continuing to work in the well-paid Belgian mining sector. The real pay differentials between Belgium and the home country are immense. Someone who earns the equivalent of 200 Belgian francs (BF) per day in Morocco as a skilled worker can get 2,000 BF per day in Belgium. And the social benefits one enjoys in Belgium simply do not exist in the home region.

Ethnic Continuity: A Rewarding Form of Identification

For many immigrants, then, employment in Belgium means a social promotion in their home country that would otherwise be inconceivable. Still, guest-workers who compare themselves socially with Belgians almost always come out losers. There remains, for first-generation workers, at least, a social gulf between them and most Belgians, quite apart from economic and financial differences. First-generation immigrants thus have every interest in maintaining continuity with their ethnic origin and their past. They can evaluate their own success against the social norms of their home region or of the immigrant community in which they live. And while doing this (and forced by circumstances to do so) they remain Turks, Berbers, or Sicilians and are not inclined to apply for Belgian naturalization. An immigrant who wants to remain acceptable in his or her home culture—and enjoy the prestige there that comes with economic success—is compelled to observe a minimal cultural model. For Muslims, of course, the model is composed of religious elements as well as of other cultural items, and Islamic customs will not likely disappear from European immigrant circles in the near future.

Orientation of first-generation immigrants to their country of origin is expressed most clearly in their insistence that they will one day return there. Social rejection by their hosts, and public commitment to their own culture and to their country of origin, gives first-generation immigrants little reason to immerse themselves in the language and culture of their host country or even to establish intensive contact with their Belgian colleagues at work. The social separation between Belgians and guest-workers is maintained by both camps.

The Unifying Process of Material Production

The process of cultural change is inexorable. Immigrants may preserve their own sense of ethnic identity and may hold on to certain key cultural values and cultural emblems, but this observable culture is significantly modified in the host country nonetheless. One factor that strongly affects the culture of immigrants, particularly if they come from rural areas, is that in Belgium they mostly live in cities. Furthermore, they work at jobs that entail direct and prolonged interaction with members of their host culture. People from Turkey, Morocco, and the rural areas of Italy, Spain, and Portugal may be accustomed to working with members of their extended families or, for the execution of certain jobs, with neighbors and friends (Cammaert, 1985; Leman, 1982; Gailly, 1983; Gailly, Hermans, and Leman, 1983). In Belgium, the culture of work is, of course, quite different. It requires collegial effort with social strangers, and assumes no need for personal allegiance among workmates. It involves assumptions about regularity of job effort (the so-called work rhythm), devotion to one's job, and promptness of job execution. It entails certain attitudes toward superiors in the company and an easy familiarity with the special vocabulary of one's trade or career. No immigrant can ignore these elements for long and hope to be successful economically. At most, worker immigrants can say that they are just going through the cultural motions in their host country—that they are using the host culture temporarily to make money and to return home to establish a business there in their own style, among their own people.

In the beginning of their career abroad, immigrants may have difficulty adapting to the new "labor culture." In rural Turkey and Morocco, for example, a man may not be considered "wasting time" if he spends hours talking to his friends at the market or in a tea house, even on an ordinary workday (Gailly, 1983; Roosens, 1979a). The daily tasks of the subsistence economy are often done by women. Men sometimes have to do heavy labor, but then generally only for short periods of time. In these rural communities there is always "tomorrow," and the days that follow, but hardly a future that one has to or even can plan for beforehand (Bourdieu, 1978). And ideas like competition in work and job performance per time unit are alien to those cultures.

Cultural conflict or no, the immigrant laborer or the small, self-employed immigrant entrepreneur has little choice: he is exposed to and must conform to the demands of the job seven to eight hours every working day

(Bovenkerk, Eijken, and Teerlink, 1983; Martens, 1973). Either he bends and adapts to the system or he loses his job. Most migrants probably realize that competition on the worldwide labor market does not permit any significant deviation from the system of cultural traits that are proper to modern production: whoever does not work long, hard, and precisely cannot compete with the Japanese or South Koreans or other industrious peoples and will disappear from the stage.

Cultural Emblems of Ethnic Belonging

Migrant culture thus undergoes major change. Eventually, only key cultural traits become moral or ethical imperatives and are seen as being of absolute importance. A Sicilian or Turkish father, for example, may insist that he has the say in the marriage of his daughter and that only he can give her away in marriage if he is to remain an honorable man. Not only has he internalized such norms as a part of himself but he must also respect them if he wants to maintain or enhance his prestige in the immigrant community. It is generally these cultural imperatives that are called "our" or "my" culture in everyday language. These cultural changes detract not at all from ethnic self-awareness. In fact, the changes may even enhance it.

"Domestic Foreigners"

The labor migrants to northern Europe of the 1960s and 1970s thus differ in many respects from immigrants to the United States and Canada of the late nineteenth and early twentieth centuries who went with the intention of settling there if the enterprise succeeded at all. Many emigrants who left for the New World very quickly gave up the idea of ever returning to the region of their birth, if they had thought to do so, and adapted themselves to America culturally, without forgetting their personal past. The United States was, in fact, largely an immigrant country and remains so to this day: except for the Native Americans and a number of Chicanos, all the inhabitants are descendants of imported blacks or of immigrants, or are themselves first-generation immigrants. And although there may be a nucleus of families who consider themselves to be *the* Americans, the United States has always been a country that has considered immigration normal (Farley, 1982). In present-day California, for example, there are people who came from dozens of countries and cultural traditions; the original American Indian population has almost vanished. A new immigrant to California from Latin America or from Asia today arrives in a culture that is totally different from the already long-established populations and traditions of Europe, traditions that may even include conflict between indigenous groups within the same state.

Brussels, the so-called capital of Europe, has for years known tensions between the French-speaking and the Dutch-speaking residents. The Dutch speakers comprise only 20% of Brussels. There are districts in the city in which more than half of the population are immigrants, and it is generally assumed that they will vote "French" should they ever be enfranchised. It is not so easy for the local population to accept that they have to live with "foreigners" who wish to retain that status but still participate in determining the political fate of the natives and even occupy positions in the municipal government. It is difficult for the native, host population to categorize this new kind of "domestic foreigner."

THE SECOND GENERATION

Cultural Assimilation

For the second generation, though, things are much clearer. Reference to the country of origin is, for most of these young people, virtually nil. Members of the second generation are unambiguously oriented to the country in which they were born and raised. The few tourist visits that they make to the region where their parents came from cannot change their orientation in most cases.

From the standpoint of observable culture, members of the second generation of guest-worker migrants in Belgium look much like the "native" youth and young adults of the country. In many ways, of course, these second-generation youth *are* natives. As they pass through the Belgian school system, the migrant children are not only forced to speak and write French and/or Dutch, but they also study in this language. Recently, in some countries of the EEC, classes have been introduced in the traditional language and culture of migrants, but in general the children from minority groups are compelled to fit the local school pattern (Foyer-Stuurgroep Bi-Cultureel, 1983; Gailly and Leman, 1982; Heyerick, 1985; Roosens, 1979c; van den Berg-Eldering, de Rijcke, and Zuck, 1983). Numerous scholarly publications, conferences, and articles in the mass media have pointed out that if immigrant children fall significantly behind in their curriculum because of inappropriate teaching, this could give rise to difficult problems. Several detailed anthropological studies have shown that many migrant children, under the influence of the school and their peers, come to see the life-style and values of their parents as dated and backward. This does not necessarily mean that the immigrant children openly break with their parents or are in conflict with them more than native children are in conflict with *their* parents, but the stresses are real enough.

It may appear that minority children will assimilate because the world of industrialized Europe appears more "modern," attractive, promising, and prestigious than the world of their parents. But it seems to me rather arbitrary to contend that people change their culture primarily because of curriculum content and the attitudes of their teachers and peers in school. Instead, it is highly probable that we are watching a worldwide process in which the material products of the West (luxury automobiles, television sets, recreational apparatus, and clothing) and the personal freedom that the youth enjoy, all attract young people. No classes in Turkish or Italian, no bicultural lessons in Belgian public schools, will change that. It is simply that items produced in the West are, from the utilitarian standpoint, better than what are found elsewhere, and that, given a choice, youth will choose personal freedom over strict obedience to parental control.

Social Isolation

But these same immigrant youths who embrace Western cultural products and norms face a rude shock. In a further phase of their development, after they move on from basic schooling and seek work and recreational opportunities, they feel very soon and very strongly that they are not fully accepted by the dominant society. Their own peers from school may even reject them outright. The most pressing issue is that of employment, and the Belgian-born sons and daughters of immigrants are not given equal opportunities. They belong overwhelmingly to a category of people of which the present economy has no need (Marangé and Lebon, 1982). Among many second-generation immigrants, there is a return to ethnic roots, what Leman (1982) has called a second migration. It is obvious that nobody can return to a "former culture" that they never had. Young adults who have resolutely grown away from the cultural environment of their early youth can simulate their traditional culture, but they are never completely at home again in what they have left. If the first migration was a transition from a rural culture, with little education, to an urban civilization based on universal public and secular education, there is no real turning back for the second generation, no matter how dejected they may feel about their social and economic isolation in the dominant society.

Psychosocial Return to the Ethnic Group

Consciously returning to "one's own people" can be accomplished in several ways. Actually going back to the home region of the parents is, of course, a radical form of remigration. Young people can indeed find the culture of their parents, but it will be a culture that has evolved and is now different from the culture of the migrants in the host country. Furthermore, everybody knows that the economic opportunities are not outstanding in the countries that send millions of guest-workers to northern Europe, and that the social security systems in those countries are generally much poorer, too. Young people who have been raised in an urban or semiurban milieu and who have assimilated the life values and style of their host country do not easily return to a rural zone where they feel themselves to be foreigners, even though members of their family live there. It is easier to return to an urban center in the country of one's parents because in all the cities of the world many elements of Western culture have been welcomed, or at least have seeped in. But for a person of the second generation this still means a step into the unknown.

Throughout northern Europe, the return to the "home region" is a theme sounded more by some members of the dominant society than by minority members themselves. For the host countries, remigration is a way to get rid of a problem. It seems apparent that many native Belgians, for example, in these difficult economic times, see remigration as an expeditious solution. I do not mean to imply that most citizens of the host countries would wish or even tolerate the violent deportation of non-EEC guest-workers. But if the repatriation could take place in a "humane" and "soft" way without evoking memories of World War II, large portions of the dominant population would probably consent to it. Although little detailed research has been done on the subject, one gets the impression from remarks made in passing that the inhabitants of northwestern Europe see no advantages in living together with "foreigners," and certainly not when these foreigners want to stay foreign, clinging to their own nationality, their own language, and their own cultural style. In those parts of Europe with the longest immigration tradition, there may be more openness to the presence of immigrants who adapt and fit in, particularly if the immigrants come from a European country. But even in the regions with the longest experience, the so-called multicultural world-of-tomorrow is not seen as an attractive opportunity for human enrichment.

The fact that many immigrants and their children do not actively assimilate is cited by pressure groups or political parties as evidence of the "degenerate" character of the minorities. By the use of symbols and simplistic statements and false reasoning, racist groups try to convince the dominant society that the minorities must go. In particular, those minorities who differ phenotypically from the majority are the targets of these campaigns (Plenel and Rollat, 1984; *Cahiers de sociologie*, 1984). Racist propaganda suggests, and often frankly states, that there are inferior and superior groups, and that the inferior affect the superior adversely by living on the same territory. Physical and genetic characteristics are merged in the racist discourse with "culture" and ethnic identity so that the "others" are rejected in their totality and on the basis of "natural," unchangeable characteristics. In order to make their objectives acceptable and to salvage a veneer of humanity, the leaders of these racist movements generally qualify their statements when they appear before the public at large. But in some countries, like France, racist phenomena such as the Le Pen party are very visible. When slogans aimed at the "foreigners" yield votes, even the established political parties will sometimes take more or less camouflaged xenophobic positions (Thränhardt, 1985). Nobody would argue that there are no problems to be solved regarding the implantation of minorities in our countries but, interestingly, first-generation immigrants who adapt only minimally and do not want to become German, Dutch, or Belgian are not the objects of personal attack. Sooner or later, it is reasoned, they are going back to their countries of origin. Thus, they are seen as a problem that will be resolved in the natural course of time. Many members of the dominant society would like it to be so, but the chance is very small that the mass of second- and third-generation minorities will return to the countries of their parents or grandparents. Meanwhile, they stay, refuse to petition for naturalization, demand that their own language be used in public education, and expect the right to vote, even if only in local elections. In fact, what is happening now is neither a massive geographic remigration nor complete assimilation to the culture of the surrounding majority.

The immigrants who cannot be distinguished phenotypically from the majority can "disappear" in public and even at work without becoming totally assimilated. The individual can live several lives, including one in a closed family circle independent of his or her public circles of acquaintances. According to Leman (1984), many young adult Italians disappear in mass public life in Belgium, while they maintain some degree of Italian life-style at home. Second-generation Italians can do this without any "technical" problems for they truly control all the necessary elements of both cultures. They fit almost perfectly into the host country, and there is little chance that they will become a source of conflict. For as long as they remain publicly invisible and are not obvious foreigners, they do not at all disturb the political and cultural perceptions of the locals.

Some young people, however, who could just as easily remain in the background, intentionally make themselves obviously visible as members of another culture. They present themselves with "aggressive ethnicity" (Leman, 1982). These are young people who perceive their own situation clearly and have accurately gauged the migration story of the guest-workers, their parents. They have largely adopted the cultural pattern of the dominant society. In no way can they appeal to substantive continuity with the objective culture of their parents or with the region of origin of their parents. They do have the artifact of descent, perhaps some phenotypical characteristics, and a limited number of cultural elements, such as their own language or their manner of conceiving friendship. But they may add to this objective continuity other elements that they create or borrow from others. Young people of Sicilian origin, for example, will cite as belonging to their own past or culture, the political success of Roman antiquity or the current achievements of great Italian authors or movie directors. At the same time, they may form an association to purchase land in Sicily and thus create a highly emotional symbol as a group possession. The rallying songs that are sung leave no doubt that what is happening is a creative reconstitution, that a past is being transformed so that it can present a unique image for the present. This is ethnogenesis—the development and public presentation of a self-conscious ethnic group.

There is nothing to indicate that if one had been given the opportunity to know one's culture of origin better—for example, by more education about that culture and in the language of that culture—more use would be made of "objective" elements than is now the case. It could well be that the past would be manipulated to the same degree. Nevertheless, it is understandable why members of the second generation now think they have been robbed of a part of their culture by the dominant school system and why they believe that things would have been different if the "cultural uniqueness" of migrant children had been respected. This feeling that the dominant society has taken something away that can never be recovered is, of itself, significant.

TRYING TO SHAPE A "MULTICULTURAL SOCIETY"

The "Migrant Question" in Brussels: An Explosive Issue

In 1988, a leading Flemish politician shocked many by stating in public that Brussels had irreversibly become multinational and that bicultural education should be introduced in all the schools attended by immigrant children so that their language and culture could be respected. Less visible initiatives leading to the same practical conclusion had been taken by a younger politician in 1987. These few tentative moves in the direction of a "multicultural society" were the most substantive happenings on the stage of immigrant policy in years, which is amazing considering that the population of some Brussels districts is more than 40% immigrant. Many politicians will admit in private that the best thing they can do is to keep silent about the simmering immigrant problems in Brussels, lest there be a backlash that could well get out of hand. Thus, official EEC guidelines, though agreed on by all member states, have yet to be put into practice.

The Complexity of Organizing Bicultural or Multicultural Education

When it comes to organizing bicultural education, Belgium is a particular case. As already noted above, tying language to territory has been one of the powerful tools the Flemish used to break French-speaking cultural dominance. For decades, nobody has been allowed to organize schools that use a language of instruction different from the official language of the district. Major legal problems, therefore, would accompany the organization of schools in which general subjects like mathematics, biology, and religion would be taught in Italian, Spanish, Turkish, Arabic, and so on. One could argue that this type of teaching program should be practiced in order to respect the language and cultural heritage of the children involved. But it is almost certain that all linguistic minorities would request the same privileges and go to court if their demands were not met. This could set off a new series of conflicts between the native linguistic communities and would mark the end of the "school peace," an agreement reached several years ago after a period of intense struggle that even included physical violence.

Religious differences are another major issue. Islam was recognized officially by the Belgian government in 1974, in the days of the oil crisis.

By Belgian law, this means that religious leaders and free schools organized by religious groups belonging to the officially registered religion can be subsidized by the government authorities up to almost 100%. Islamic schools attended and run by Muslims, who generally are not Belgian citizens, would thus be paid for by the Belgian taxpayers. This could turn into a major political and "racial" issue if a network of Islam schools develops. Up to the present, many Muslim parents send their children to Catholic schools, mainly because they are convinced that the Catholic school system, which comprises more than 70% of all schools in Belgium, is better academically and is not as "heathen" as the state network. For their part, though they would be free to do so, Catholic schools do not want to refuse enrollment to Muslim children for ethical reasons. It is felt that if Muslim parents ask for admission on their own initiative, Muslim children should be admitted and due respect should be paid to their religious beliefs. In Brussels, and also in a few other Belgian cities, more than 50% of the school population of many Catholic schools is Muslim, and in some schools more than 90%. Nevertheless, the organization of courses in Islam by Catholic schools, as a part of the official curriculum, is deemed impracticable for several reasons.

First of all, it would not be accepted by the Belgian public as a matter of principle that one and the same confessional school would teach two competing world religions. Moreover, and this is even more important, the Catholic network of schools has the right to found and maintain its own schools, with its own selected personnel, *because* this sort of freedom has been claimed and enforced by Catholic citizens who want their religion and educational style to be respected. Furthermore, although it might sound bizarre to outsiders, this situation does not eliminate courses in Catholicism from being taught in the official public schools of cities, provinces, and the state. The general reasoning that underlies this rather amazing situation is that taking courses in the Catholic religion does not guarantee that a person will acquire a Catholic perspective in all aspects of life. For example, "neutral" teachers of history in state schools *could* subtly undo what religion teachers try to build, it is reasoned.

There is more. Official (that is, public) schools are required by law to organize courses in any recognized religion if a certain minimum number of parents request it. These regulations make it virtually impossible for Catholic (that is, private but nearly fully subsidized) schools to organize courses in Islamic religion. Such an initiative would not only compromise the Catholic character of the school and contradict the logic of the system but would also unleash the criticism of the competing state schools, which have been given the task of meeting the needs of the non-Catholic minorities.

This issue is particularly thorny because the decline in the school population threatens to bring about a drastic reduction of teaching positions in the near future and because one out of every two children born in the city of Brussels is a child of immigrant parents.

A State-Subsidized Muslim Educational Network?

It would seem logical for Muslim organizations to found their own schools for their own children. The Belgian government would be legally required to subsidize these schools, provided they met official academic and administrative standards. Some Catholic bishops are encouraging such a development, with a view to protecting the Catholic character of their own schools. This issue is also important for a number of Catholic parents who object to the presence of so many Muslim children in the Catholic schools where their own children are being educated. On the other hand, Catholic teachers fear losing their jobs if Muslim schools are established.

It is clear, then, that the creation of a generalized system of bicultural education is not a simple issue. But there are still other questions involved that make the task of organizing cultural and ethnic continuity extremely complicated, especially in the case of the Turkish and Moroccan groups. There is first of all the problem of meeting academic standards. Theoretically speaking, Muslim organizing committees would be free to select and appoint their own school staff. It would be impossible, however, to find enough competent staff within the immigrant communities. Therefore, teachers would have to be imported from the respective countries of origin. This is a potential source of trouble. Generally speaking, staff trained in the home country would not be familiar with Belgian standards of education, which are considered exceptionally high. Furthermore, staff would be suspect in the eyes of the ethnic minorities in Belgium: a number of these people could well be spies, sent by the repressive political regimes of the homeland.

The Danger of Apartheid

There is still another question to be considered. If Muslim children are educated in separate schools, there is a good chance that they will not be prepared to live in a multiethnic society. Nor, for that matter, would the majority of Belgian children. Thus, separate schooling is likely to produce a separatist type of society. And even worse: minority people educated in

Muslim schools might well encounter insuperable problems when they enter the labor market, which is dominated by members of the Fleming and Walloon communities. It is not inconceivable that Muslim schools would be considered backward by the Belgian population at large, especially as Islam enforces some moral rules regarding the position of women and the sexual education of youth—rules perceived as obsolete and "medieval" by the surrounding majority.

Some European experts on Islam hope that serious conflicts between Muslims and the majority can be avoided by encouraging the development of some sort of urbanized, European Muslim groups, similar to the Jewish communities that live among the majority without major problems. Whatever future developments there may be, these experts see the expansion of Islamic communities in northwestern Europe as inevitable, and research in this field is confirming their expectations. Islam will become a visible reality in the coming years (Dassetto, 1988). The recent explosion of the number of mosques and Islamic associations has been spectacular in France (Kepel, 1987), and Belgium is witnessing a similar phenomenon. As far as we can see from our own field research, the first-generation Muslim immigrants have been faithful to their religion, and many of the second generation in Belgium identify more and more with Islam, partly as a means of social identification. Religious membership subsumes ethnic belonging in such a way that the stigma of belonging to a Turkish or Moroccan subclass vanishes and is replaced by a more prestigious emblem. Although not very much cherished by European natives, Islam is still a world power, whereas the Turkish or Moroccan proletariat is not. Thus, emphasizing Islamic membership becomes a means of social promotion for immigrant workers and their families. Islam is not only officially recognized and subsidized by the Belgian state, and, as such, is a protected organization, it is also funded by the wealthier oil countries. According to well-informed insiders, Brussels, as a central location in Europe and as the potential capital of the continent after the 1992 consolidation of the EEC countries, may be one of the favored spots where Islamic power will try to establish itself in Europe. It is noteworthy that Islam has made a certain number of converts among the Belgian population, and that Flemish Muslims are henceforth a reality.

Broadening the Experimental Phase in Bicultural Education

Although political decisions are risky business in the present circumstances, tentative steps are being taken in line with the official theory. In

July 1988, the Flemish government decided that experiments in bicultural education should be extended to a larger number of schools in the Brussels area, where they began a few years ago. If this expanded experiment is successful, this type of education would be generalized to the Flemish region of Belgium. The formula selected was devised by "Foyer," an umbrella organization supervising a number of initiatives in the Brussels migration areas. This model of education is set up so that young children gradually switch from the parents' language to *two* other local languages, starting from kindergarten, so that they are *trilingual* (their own language, Flemish, and French) in a quite acceptable way when they leave the *primary school* by age 12. The system has been evaluated by independent experts and is considered to be a true success.

Bi- and Trilingualism: A Considerable Asset

The philosophy behind this formula is quite simple: being educated in their own language, with respect for their own cultural origin, children are not alienated by learning other languages and realities; in fact, they achieve better than if they were forced to operate in one school language only. Over the years, the immigrant children are increasingly put together with children from local communities and take the same courses, so that harmonious social relations have a chance to develop. Being trilingual constitutes a considerable asset in a unifying Europe, where even the citizens of the "big nations," such as France and Great Britain, are beginning to experience their monolingual education as a handicap.

Generalizing bi- or tricultural education is not a simple task, however, even if one is fully prepared to do so. As in all immigration countries of Western Europe, trained teaching staff is lacking. So is experience and knowledge. The very first university course on bicultural education, to which experts from all over Europe have been contributing, was started at the University of Leuven with government subsidies in 1987. It became obvious very quickly that only a small number of the most motivated teachers (university graduates with a great deal of teaching experience) succeeded in grasping what communicating with people from other cultures entails. After more than 18 months of weekly meetings, we did not succeed in breaking the monocultural Flemish setting in which most of the participants continued to encapsulate themselves, their excellent motivation notwithstanding.

EMERGING EUROPE:
ETHNIC RELATIONS OF AN ORIGINAL NATURE

The idea that local, native majorities should invest considerable amounts of human and material resources in systems of education to meet the needs of immigrants who want to keep their own cultural tradition, who cling to their own ethnic identity, and who refuse to naturalize may not be entirely new in human history. But it could take on a particular meaning in the Europe of the late 1980s and early 1990s.

To start with, the major immigrant groups in France, Great Britain, The Netherlands, Germany, and Belgium come from countries with widely divergent histories and which display a marked variety in the nature of their respective relationships to the immigration countries involved. All of these countries have been supplying varying numbers of EEC immigrants for decades. But even for the citizens of a country like The Netherlands, which declared itself to be an "immigration country" in 1981, it remains a solid fact that the different nations of Europe are experienced by almost all citizens and political leaders as distinct cultural realities. Very few Britons know any foreign language; the same applies to the French. Britain can be confident that its language is the dominant world language, while France is trying to demonstrate that French and *la Francité* are still important. Germany is much more open to foreign languages, especially English. The Netherlands, and especially the Flemish-speaking part of Belgium, are more flexible in language matters by tradition. Nevertheless, the cultural diversity of Europe remains a strong and deeply-rooted reality. The efforts migrants, or even tourists, show in adapting to the local language and culture is perceived in terms of respect and underlying social hierarchy. Nonadaptation, after years of living as an immigrant, is seen as evidencing either a sense of superiority or as sheer stupidity.

Organizing education in a foreign language and about a foreign culture on one's own soil for the benefit of ethnic minorities who left the lower economic strata of their country of origin implies an unaccustomed degree of "stooping" or "bowing." The soil of the country is still the soil of the autochthons, not merely a part of Europe. There is no unifying language, nor will there be one in the foreseeable future. Even the national enmities of World War II have not been entirely forgotten.

The idea of organizing minority cultures becomes even more questionable when it concerns minorities coming from former colonies, as is the case in Great Britain, The Netherlands, and France. Colonies, by definition, were considered parts of the world to be "civilized." Britain and France, in particular, as major colonial powers, have successfully imposed their language and culture on huge parts of the world. In the opinion of many, it is almost unthinkable that these former colonial powers would be willing to spend effort and money in order to grant linguistic and cultural facilities to former colonial subjects on the very soil of the former colonial "motherland." This would come close to inverting—some even might think perverting—history.

Islam was the former enemy of Christian Europe, so while the immigrants claim the right to stay where they are and to retain their language, religion, and other trappings of their culture, the native people of industrialized Europe feel they are being asked to adapt to the needs of an underclass minority, and even to subsidize Islam. This is not, of course, attractive to local people. Some experts even fear that Muslims will not respond to "tolerance" with equally open-minded generosity.

In our material, the Belgian case, as a part of the European scene, is unique. In Belgium, the question is raised of granting rights to ethnic minorities who, like the Moroccans and the Turks, have no real power. This creates a new type of ethnic relations. In most cases I know of, the minorities who keep their own cultural traditions and peoplehood succeed in doing so because they fund it with their own resources, like many Jewish minorities; or because they can claim some kind of restitution, like the Hurons; or because they fight for it, physically, like the Luba. Up to now, the failure to implement the guidelines and recommendations of the EEC authorities regarding the incorporation of cultures is due precisely to this lack of "convincing" power or potential impact of the minorities. When insiders say that nothing serious will be achieved before "something happens" from the immigrants side—meaning some form of terrorism or urban guerrilla movement—they point to the same lack of power.

If, however, some form of truly multicultural setting could materialize under the present conditions, it could become a unique phenomenon: strong but peaceful ethnic self-awareness could go hand in hand with dynamic cultural continuity fed by the countries of origin, which, unlike other sources of tradition in many other cases of ethnicity, are still vital. The "United States of Europe"—if such an entity ever develops—might be very different from the United States of America in terms of ethnic relations.

-10-

FINAL REFLECTIONS
Ethnic Subtleties

ETHNIC IDENTITY IN PLURAL FORM

Our Belgian–European material alone shows that there is no single, uniform process of ethnogenesis. Consequently, ethnic belonging and interethnic relations come in different shapes. For example, first-generation immigrants belong to the ethnic category "Turk" or "Moroccan" in a different way than do their Belgian-born sons and daughters. And the children of migrants who "pass" successfully in public life while staying Italians or Spaniards in the privacy of their homes, are a different case. Moreover, those who by their own choice vanish entirely in the mainstream constitute a particular new category of Flemings, Walloons, or Brusselers. Being a Muslim in Brussels can reinforce ethnic belonging as a psychological reality while concealing ethnic identification at the social level. Further, Brussels embodies only one particular type of setting: the Brussels scenario reflects the ethos of an industrialized, nonimmigration country. In a global context it is quite different from an immigration area like contemporary California.

Add to the Brussels scene the ambiguity of the Aymara of Turco, the recent birth of the so-called African "traditional tribes" of the Luba and the Luluwa, and the shades and shadows of Huron ethnicity, and one can easily understand that ethnic phenomena are direly massacred and misunderstood, if ethnicity is reduced "in essence" to a form of class struggle or to merely a symptom of plain backwardness. The variety of processes and meanings we have been documenting constitute, in their own right, an integral part of a complex reality. No deep understanding or explanation is possible without a painstaking reconstitution, case by case. Neither can one leave out the concrete, particularizing results of the individual cases from the elaboration of a comparative study.

Nevertheless, recurrent patterns do exist, and in what follows, I will try to synthesize some recurrent dimensions. I will not draw any sweeping conclusions. My theoretical propositions go just as far as the empirical material

149

reaches. As I mentioned in the first chapter of this book, I will concentrate here on two questions that are clearly documented by the presented material and have somewhat been neglected in recent theory: (1) What happens to "objective culture' in ethnic interaction, and how is "objective culture," as an active principle, affecting the process of ethnogenesis? (2) Is there any underlying force that explains why a number of material products, flowing from advanced science and technology, are transculturally perceived as superior, and how is this perception affecting the cultural form of ethnicity?

ETHNIC STRUGGLE IN CULTURAL FORM: CONDITIONS

Ethnicity, Acculturation, and Power Relationships

The intentional instrumental use of the right to one's own "objective culture," of cultural identity, of ethnic self-respect, and of the right to continued experience as a people, and the use of terms such as "ethnocide," "genocide," and "cultural imperialism"—which characterize only one form of ethnic expression (Horowitz, 1985)—seem to me, at least for the cases studied here, to be products of Western culture and particular relations between peoples on the world level.

In order to see and use one's own culture as a right, one must first have gained distance from that culture. In other words, one must first have questioned it or it must have been questioned by a process of forced acculturation: by the intervention, for example, of a colonizer who, by means of all kinds of seductive procedures, by the imposition of educational programs, and by the propagation of an ideology of the "civilization," causes the initial local culture largely to disappear and imposes a dominant culture of Western origin. People who fully or to a large extent still live in the rather stable traditional culture in which they are born know, as a rule, no other cultural system nor have they developed distance with respect to their own civilization. Their culture is, for them, something that is proper, that is, a set of morals, something that is so willed by Allah, God, or some other higher being and thus is and will remain unchangeable. In other words, the nonreflected culture manifests itself immediately in the form of moral prescriptions and rituals. For this reason, in the past—and today still in countries with a low degree of cultural reflexivity—"religious wars" would flare up, or struggles for "moral values" of a clearly particularistic kind, or

simply battles or wars for one or another piece of territory. At least some
leaders must have gone to the West via an acculturation process or an
assimilation process before an ethnic struggle could occur in terms of *the
right to one's own culture.* And a substantial part of the population must
also have gained one or another form of cultural relativistic insight before
political movements of any size could be launched.

The Aymara of Bolivia have not reached this degree of reflexive
knowledge of their own culture. This is also true of the married North
African Berber women of the first generation of immigrants in Belgium.
They see the prestigious products of the "modern" world as something
from which they are still very far removed but which they still want to have
for themselves. The Aymara of Turco, who also have experienced cultural
continuity to a high degree, which does not mean that their culture has remained unchanged, were in 1975–1980 completely oriented to urbanization and to "progress" and "economic development." Ethnic struggle in
terms of culture was totally absent, and "traditional" culture was even
destroyed from the inside.

On the other hand, the Hurons of Quebec, who are almost completely
acculturated and assimilated, including their language and production modes,
consider their own cultural tradition, insofar as there are still clear traces
of it, largely from the outside. This also is the case with the second-
generation southern Italians in Belgium, who have been educated in the local
Dutch or French curricula, and especially for those among them who have
attended secondary or higher schools. Their education has created a great
distance between them and the culture of their parents. This process is only
incipiently present among the second-generation, younger Moroccan women
or girls who work or study in Belgium. The school system, as it functions
in Belgium, by forcing young people to speak the local language and to
attend classes to learn and study in that language, seems to be a quite effi-
cient way of creating a perspective on cultural differences, even if the
children only attend primary school or a few years of secondary school.
The home culture becomes an "object" to the children: they see it at a
certain distance, and at the same time realize what is meant by the demand
for the preservation of one's own culture and one's own ethnic identity.

This creates a paradox, for the ethnic claims and slogans are mainly formulated by people who seem to have markedly moved away from their own
culture of origin, which they want to "keep." Seeing one's culture "from
the outside" does not imply, however, that one can no longer be authentic
or truthful when claiming the right to keep one's own tradition. Tradition

then becomes an object of a choice, which can be more conscious and intentional than would be possible if this distance had not been created. The notion of "cultural authenticity," such as used by skeptical, purist outsiders looking with suspicion on what they perceive as "fake ethnic groups and feelings," is grounded in the idea that genuine ethnic identity requires immersion in some pure, intact lifestyle or culture. When seen from the point of view of the people whose authenticity is put in doubt, this way of defining other ethnic groups from the outside can be perceived as aggression, a kind of imposition of heteronomy that touches the very roots of self-definition. Numerous passages in this book leave no doubt that strong ethnic feelings need not be based on a strong "objective" cultural continuity. In the cases studied here, the contrary prevails.

Cultural Relativism as a Perspective of the Actor

The second condition for the "ethnic struggle" is the presence, somewhere (in casu, this is in the West) of a mature and developed corpus of ideas regarding cultural relativism. This, of course, is more than the condition that results from being bereft of one's own cultural tradition. The ideas about cultural relativism were developed in social and cultural anthropology in the 1930s, and the theme has since been treated elsewhere (Lemaire, 1976; Roosens, 1979d). This body of ideas has fully penetrated the conceptual world of a broader mass of politicians, journalists, authors, academicians, and many layers of the working population only after World War II, particularly after the 1960s. The victory over Nazi Germany and the worldwide revulsion at what the Jewish people had suffered led to the propagation of international manifestos and proclamations regarding racism, the right to identity, and so on. The decolonization of Asia, Africa, and elsewhere also gave concrete form to a kind of vulgarized cultural relativism, although this recognition has remained limited as regards content. After the Second Vatican Council, another attitude developed in many religious circles and communities toward other religions, at least in theory.

In my opinion, the vulgarized form of cultural relativism is just as much a product of shifted power relationships as it is of an intellectual and moral current that was already present in the West and that gave this shifting of relations an ideological form. It seems to me a great oversimplification to see cultural relativism as the product of a kind of "internal" or "moral" growth of humanity, free of influence from social confrontations, wars, mass murders, and rebellious leaders of peoples in the colonized world.

Cultural relativism is a product of all this and not exclusively or not even primarily of an inspired, voluntary, and selfless conversion of the West.

The brand of relativism that was developed in many disciplines both in Europe and in the United States reflected a particular ideology and influenced many people from other cultures as well. At least officially, cultural relativism has become a basis for the development of relations with the post colonial West, for all the countries of the world officially agree that every people must be able to determine the content of its own culture in a free manner.

"Culture": A Useful Weapon in Peaceful Settings

Unarmed struggle in terms of culture, moreover, requires a real democratic climate in the global community where this struggle is conducted. In this sense it is, politically speaking, a conflict in a deluxe form. For it implies that the dominant majority is, in one way or another, receptive, albeit under moral pressure, to make at least some concessions, and that it refrains from using its physical–military superiority. The Congo at the time of its independence did not meet this condition. In countries with a highly repressive dictatorial regime, one does not fight in terms of "cultural identity." There one opposes or rebels against economic exploitation, corruption of the authorities, or political oppression. In such contexts, peaceful movements have only a minimum chance of success.

"Culture Struggle": A Problem of Wealthy States

The "cultural" struggle also assumes a significant degree of prosperity in the global society. The "minority" must be able to act against the administration of the welfare state, either as an internal group contained in a welfare state or as an external proletariat, as a Third World country versus a former colonizer or a great power. It is typical that the dominant opponent is always a country or the administration of a country with a Western culture. This does not seem to me to be a matter of chance. For the West has what others would also wish to have—social security, comfort, all kinds of products, prestige, luxury, intellectual insights, and technological mastery in many domains—in spite of all the ideologies that contend otherwise.

Culture and Power

It does not seem to be advantageous, however, to demand modern conveniences in the name of ethnic equality just because one is poor and of another culture. In this case, "equality" does not work. The protest and demands of the Hurons have not been heard for centuries. And the present-day Turks and Moroccans in Belgium or Germany are voiceless because they have no muscle. Ironically, claims must be formulated by people who are already equals in some way and who have power. Along these same lines, one can actively promote one's case by projecting a positive image, as do many Indians of North America. Indeed, they have succeeded in becoming popular in many parts of the world, which has considerably increased their power. There is no evidence of comparable sympathy for foreign workers in Europe—they have a negative profile and are merely a problem. The Indians also have their problems. Many live in miserable conditions, and alcoholism seems to be a destructive plague on many reservations. Objectively, most Indians are much worse off than most foreign workers in Belgium. But these aspects are kept out of the picture. The Indians also have the "advantage" of having been the object of involuntary colonization and of living on their own territory, while the foreign workers are "voluntary" immigrants and thus allochthons. Moreover, the culture of most of the immigrants has nothing appealing about it: it is a workers' culture. A "tribe" of Indians, for its part, is believed to have an entirely original culture, common to all the Indians of that particular group without any class distinction. This gives them a noble cachet.

STRATEGIC ADVANTAGES OF CULTURAL IDENTITY
IN ETHNIC RELATIONS

The Prehensile Openness of Culture

The concept of cultural relativism—to a large extent a Western product—also permits the dominated culture to be presented in such a way that it becomes reconcilable with the fruits of modern technology. It is stressed that a living culture never stands still and that the particular culture is of the open type; one is always prepared to learn from others and to adopt what seems useful or desirable after a critical examination. The minorities are forced to adopt such a definition and behave accordingly, otherwise they would be at odds with their demands for the transfer of material or technological resources. As far as I know, it is only very exceptional for a people to continue to lock themselves voluntarily in their traditional culture when they have the opportunity to go outside it and to acquire the technology of the West.

The Elasticity of Culture and History

Culture is a "reality" that can be elastic; even in professional circles, one can find more than a hundred definitions of "culture." When speaking of one's "own culture" and the continuity in this "own culture," one has many options because the symbolic transformations that former life ways, values, and so forth can undergo are virtually limitless. One can always say that innovative creativity keeps a culture vital and thus nothing inauthentic lurks in it. One only becomes vulnerable when certain reconstitutions are presented as "actually having happened," as "really true," when this is not the case.

The same also applies to "history" or "the past." These two dimensions overlap when cultural tradition, by its nature, concerns the past. For many groups, their critical knowledge of the facts of the past is so faulty that a great many "reconstitutions of facts" are quite possible. When one then wants to assign a certain meaning to the past (for example, "the discovery of America was in fact the beginning of emigration to the West of people who disturbed the peace everywhere, polluted the environment, and exploited other groups of people and not a beneficial 'pilgrimage of civilization': the whites are thus unwelcome and late-arrivals on American territory"), many courses are available. Moreover, assigning meaning to the past also poses a problem for professional historians. It is certain that the meaning that one ultimately will give to the past is partially determined by one's present *Sitz im Leben*.

What, finally, applies in a given period as "reality," and thus what is taken into account, is what can be reciprocally obtained in the present constellation of interethnic power relations. These power relations themselves can be partially determined by a large number of "external" factors, such as the pressure of international opinion. But what is accepted by all parties involved presents itself, after a certain time, as a "given."

THE OBJECTIVE CORE OF HUMAN CONSTRUCTION

Ethnic groups and their cultures are not merely a completely arbitrary construct: there is always a minimum of incontestable and noninterpretable facts necessary to win something from the opponent. This minimum is of course insufficient, but, if it is not present, there is little chance that one's interpretation will be wholly or partially accepted. Thus, the Hurons could for a time participate in a front of Indians who are claiming territory. In 1982 they were standing practically alone. They were dropped by other Indians because they no longer lived on their pre-Columbian territory. And, as the ideological background of the Indian law is beginning to show, whoever is not descended from Indians has no chance of being accepted as an Indian. The reality is very elastic but not totally arbitrary.

Thus, all of the parties accept a kind of objective truth as a possibility and as a criterion. They also present their own interpretations as "the truth." None of them would say that he or she is telling only a story or a myth. The combination in political practice of history, culture, identity, and ancestry, however, makes it possible for an indisputable fact or "truth" to be transferred from one domain to another. With very little, therefore, one can obtain very much (see, for example, Gros-Louis, 1981). Moreover, it is also possible that another dimension of the reality—such as living for generations in one and the same territory or in one and the same village— brings with it a feeling of solidarity that is transferred to other elements, such as having the same blood, in the presentation of things by the parties.

ETHNICITY AND MODERN MATERIAL RESOURCES: DIALECTICAL CHANGE

Appropriating more material resources, directly or through education, via restitution money or increased political power, is a theme that pervades all our case studies. The kind of material resources sought is invariably the same: in our cases, ethnic minorities want the latest and most sophisticated products and try to get as much as they can. Not all people act this way all of the time, but most do most of the time.

In some cases, new, modernizing material resources are claimed for the preservation of the traditional life-style. Paradoxically, human beings manipulate and even re-create or invent the old in order to attain the new in an attempt to bypass competitive achievement. Where ethnic belonging is irrelevant or counterproductive, ethnicity is minimalized or entirely hidden away, at least publicly.

In these case studies, nobody strongly identifies with his or her ethnic past if this form of identification is counterproductive. The ethnic issue never implies a return to poorer material conditions of the past. In this sense ethnicity involves not only the past but also the future, as in the case of many new religions that use "return to tradition" in order to advance more rapidly. The Cargo Cults of New Guinea are a well-known example of this, as are the thousands of new religions of black Africa. Old rites, or patterns of behavior that are presented as such, are used to reap benefits in the modern sector of life. Believers return to ancestor worship but hope that their ancestors will come back to this world as "modern," sophisticated white people, with all the wealth and material goods of modern times. Business people consult "traditional" diviners in order to maximize their profits in the market economy.

The longing for the material goods of the modern world is not random but shows a great consistency: people want things that they perceive to be of superior quality, commodities that put one in command when one uses them, objects that offer hedonic advantages and that reflect some perceived universal mental superiority. The envied material things are thus also highly symbolic for one's position in the universe. In many cases, a kind of transcultural consensus is reached about the value of a number of products of the modern world. No relativism is found here. This sphere clearly concerns the measurable, the comparable, that which falls within the realm of reason, at least as far as hedonic value and the practical advantages of material objects are concerned. It may take some time, but in the long run higher-quality goods win consensus about their worth in widely different cultures.

Ethnic Differentiation and Growing Cultural Uniformity

Consequently there is a steady movement in the various cultures toward uniformity. Strictly speaking, although material things have no meaning by themselves, they affect people who want them, possess them, work for them, or try to manipulate social relations and power structures to obtain them. To be sure, some form of specific reinterpretation takes place in each particular cultural context, but this reinterpretation is always limited when it concerns material goods.

The temptation of the world of white or "Catholic" (in the case of the Aymara) material goods leads to cultural uniformity for those who acquire and use these goods. The same is true, but to a much higher degree, for those who also produce these goods or even leave their country of origin for foreign soil in order to do so. The first-generation immigrants in Belgium clearly show cultural transformation. In the second generation, one may already speak of a true cultural mutation. Material culture, then, is never merely a material issue. Goods, once created and produced, have their own logic. An automobile or a snowmobile transforms the lifestyle of human beings. Living in a place and developing it into a town, as the Aymara do, radically changes the general atmosphere of life of a rural group. In this sense, modern material goods make lifestyles more uniform as they circulate throughout the world. Once a group decides to produce the modern goods on its own, these material objects have an immeasurable and inevitable impact: people adopt other patterns of living in order to produce and consume in a given way. And once they are producing in the new mode, sooner or later they get caught up in some form of competition and are forced into still more uniform techniques for the very good reason that the number of ways to produce profitably are limited. Making snowshoes in the traditional fashion—an ethnic emblem for Huron Indians—is five times too expensive, and thus nonviable for the Huron manufacturer. And the Indian leaders of the James Bay Convention have had to learn the methods of modern Canadian administration for similar reasons. The same is true for the first-generation immigrants in Belgium, even if they try to see and evaluate themselves in terms of their homeland.

Ethnicity and Social Equalization

In all our case studies, ethnicity has had to do with material goods, whether in a positive or negative way: the Hurons maximize their ethnicity in order to obtain resources, whereas the Aymara try to destroy their own cultural and ethnic traits for the same reason. The longing for material goods does not by itself produce ethnic identity or ethnicity. Ethnicity, however, *is* directly concerned with group formation, and thus with power relations. And it is a particular network of power relations at the world level which makes the ethnic self-affirmation of minorities respectable and useful as a tool in the distribution and redistribution of material goods. After a holocaust and decolonization the way to equalization among human groups is theoretically open. By defining oneself in ethnic terms, one escapes hierar-

Final Reflections 159

chical classification, at least on the official, public level. As contrasted with the world of material goods and technical productivity, there is no universal yardstick to be found in this realm. There is nothing with which to measure the value of the different forms or contents of ethnicity. By definition, ethnic origins must be unique, and the way they are unique is historical, not measurable. As far as peoples, nations, or ethnic groups are concerned, there are no higher or lower origins. At least this is the way people have started to think in recent times, on the public, official level after centuries of thinking, speaking, and behaving to the contrary. In the past, vast wealth was taken from many "primitive" or "underdeveloped" peoples by force and with contempt. By the same logic, this wealth can and should be returned, now that equality is recognized and established as a value among the "civilized" peoples of the world. The case of the Amerindians of Quebec is an illustration of this new conception of international or interethnic relations. The same value system dictates that immigrant minorities be given their rights to stay what they are in terms of culture and ethnic belonging while they receive equal economic opportunity so that new forms of colonization can be avoided. The first case is a question of restitution and redemption; the second a matter of prevention.

It would be one-sided, then, to see the struggle for material goods as the sole scientifically relevant issue in ethnic confrontations. Being taken seriously or being respected is a social value that has equal or even more standing in matters of ethnicity, and the claim for material goods runs through this channel of recognition and respect. In human interaction, material goods have both an instrumental and an expressive side. To return material goods one has taken away or to pay some other form of restitution is a means of honoring or recognizing the dignity of the other party. Giving "equal opportunities" or applying some form of "positive discrimination" for immigrant children is a way of recognizing them as worthy members of society. Material goods, when given and accepted, incarnate recognition and rehabilitation.

ETHNICITY AND THE CREATION OF "NATURAL" SYMBOLS

Nothing "natural" determines that ethnic self-affirmation, or claims made in terms of that self-affirmation, should be instrumental in obtaining material and socially symbolic goods. Ethnicity, as it functions today, is a phase of a long, ongoing story. Today, the mode of competitive production is imposing increasing uniformity on the peoples of the earth. At the same time, however, new technologies make leisure time and entertainment more possible than ever before. So much so that entertainment, film, television, music, radio, and the other mass media have become a gigantic production sector in themselves. In these areas, the products are largely symbolic. And though the same laws of competition and technology govern communication and art production, their products escape to a degree the homogenizing working conditions that prevail elsewhere. Some indetermination and room for culture differentiation is left here. The creation of symbols is massive, and new ways of expressive invention and cultural differentiation or restoration are opened up.

In the same perspective, political discourse, which is basically of the same nature as other forms of creative art, can use the same wealth of symbol creation and diffusion. The most successful speeches of political leaders are mostly general in nature, appealing as they do to polyvalent ethical schemes through polysemous words and bodily expressions. Ethnic political speeches, of course, are of the same nature. They have little in common with scientific treatises, especially when they deal with important issues. Nor are they well-balanced considerations taking all aspects of questions into account. Usually, they present the characteristics of the book (Gros-Louis, 1981) I analyzed in Chapter 4. History can be replayed, and so can interethnic relations. By displaying the inhuman character of Nazi anti-Semitism or of slavery, modern mass media remold feelings and relations between human groups. The descendants of former victims may gain respect and social compensation.

Ethnicity is a rich subject for the setting I just described. By its own nature, it offers a broad field for the use and manipulation of symbols. To begin with, the ingredients used in ethnic discourse seem quite natural: descent, biological origin, belonging together, land, culture, and history all seem eminently real and constitute what many people consider to be palpable realities. At the same time, they are all extremely vague in their definition. Nobody can deny that a given group of people has ancestors, that they have a past, a culture, a biological origin, or that they have been living somewhere, on some piece of land. These facts constitute the eminently solid, genuine, irreducible side of ethnicity, ethnic identity, and ethnic feelings. But who exactly these ancestors were, where they lived, what type of culture they transmitted, and the degree to which this culture was an original creation, and what their relationships were with other, similar ethnic groups in the past—all these are frequently open questions for the open mind. Political discourse and ethnic politics, of course, need not imply an open mind. And even if they do, the lack of definition of the things involved, their imprecision, their predominant arationality, make them remarkably flexible and useful as building materials for an ethnic ideology. In the ethnic arsenal you can partially forget what you know if others do not notice or do not mind. You can add things if exact knowledge is not available. You can choose a suitable variant if different theories exist. You can combine and transplant. You can inject vigor and authenticity, stemming, for example, from territorial propinquity, as the Hurons do, into feelings of "racial purity." Almost anything and everything are possible, as long as no falsehoods are told that are too obviously refuted by common knowledge and as long as the adversary is not too strong.

All this makes ethnicity exciting for people who study how social "reality" is created, maintained, and changed. Thus, although ethnicity must be distinguished from "observable or objective" culture, as I stressed, with F. Barth, at the beginning of this book, it appears, paradoxically, as a privileged domain for the study of cultural dynamics. Moreover, the study of ethnic phenomena reveals how far ethnic ideology and historical reality can diverge from each other; how much people feel things that are not there and conveniently forget realities that have existed; how people constantly take for "natural givens" what they themselves have constituted in an unconscious way.

References

Government Documents

Elimination de la discrimination selon le sexe dans la Loi sur les Indiens (1982). Ottawa: Affaires indiennes et du Nord Canada.

Historique de la Loi sur les Indiens (1980). Ottowa: Centre de recherches historiques et d'études des traités, Orientations générales, Affaires indiennes et du Nord Canada.

La Convention de la Baie James et du Nord québecois (1976). Editeur officiel du Québec.

La négociation d'un mode de vie. La structure administrative découlant de la Convention de la Baie James: L'expérience initiale des Cris (1979). Montreal, La Cité.

La nouvelle entente Québec–Canada (1979). Gouvernement du Québec.

La politique indienne du Gouvernement du Canada (Livre Blanc) (1969). Ottawa: Ministère des Affaires indiennes et du Nord Canada.

La politique québecoise du développement culturel (1978), 1. "Perspectives d'ensemble: de quelle culture s'agit-il?" 2. Les trois dimensions d'une politique: genres de vie, création, éducation." Gouvernement du Québec.

Les Indiens. Situation actuelle (1980). Ottawa: Affaires indiennes et du Nord Canada.

Les lois sur les Indiens et leurs lois modificatrices, 1868–1950 (1981). Ottawa: Centre de la recherche historique et de l'étude des traites, Orientations générales, Affaires indiennes et du Nord Canada.

Loi concernant les Indiens, Chaps. 1–6 (1970). Imprimeur de la Reine pour le Canada.

Loi sur les Indiens, Codification administrative (1978). Ministre des Approvisionnements et Services Canada.

"Nishastanan Nitasinan (Conseil Attikamek–Montagnais), Autochtones: luttes et conjonctures I" (1979). Recherches amérindiennes au Québec, 9 (3).

Rapport de la Commission d'étude sur l'intégrité du territoire du Québec (1971). 4. "Le Domaine indien"; 4.1. "Rapport des commissaires"; 4.5. "Inventaire des réserves et établissements indiens." (Rapport Dorion), Québec.

Relationes (seventeenth century). Jesuits.

General References

Aerts, M. and A. Martens (1978) Gastarbeider, lotgenoot en landgenoot? Leuven: Kritak.

Anciaux, V. (1978) Press conference of May 30, p. 48.

Banton, M. and J. Harwood (1975) The Race Concept. New York: Praeger.

Barth, F. (ed.) (1969) Ethnic Groups and Boundaries: The Social Organization of Cultural Difference. Boston: Little, Brown.

Bell, D. (1975) "Ethnicity and social change," pp. 141–174 in N. Glazer and D. Moynihan (eds.) Ethnicity: Theory and Experience. Cambridge, MA: Harvard University Press.

Boiteau, G. (1954) Les chasseurs hurons de Lorette. Quebec: Université Laval, Faculté des Lettres.

Bourdieu, P. (1978) Algérie 60. Paris: Les éditions de Minuit.

Bovenkerk, F., A. Eijken, and W. Bovenkerk-Teerlink (1983) Italiaans ijs: de opmerkelijke historie van Italianse ijsbereiders in Nederland. Meppel: Boom.

Bruner, E. (1974) "The expression of ethnicity in Indonesia," pp. 251-280 in A. Cohen (ed.) Urban ethnicity. London: Tavistock Publications.

Cahiers de sociologie et d'économie régionales (1984). Critique régionale 10-11, Recherches sur l'immigration. Brussels: Editions de l'Université de Bruxelles.

Cammaert, M.-F. (1985) Migranten en thuisblijvers: een confrontatie. De leefwereld van Marokkaanse Berbervrouwen. Leuven: University Press/Àssen. Maastricht: Van Gorcum.

Cardinal, H. (1977) The Rebirth of Canada's Indians. Edmonton: Hurtig Publishers.

Chrétien, J. (1969) La politique indienne du Gouvernement du Canada. Ottawa: Affaires indiennes et du Nord Canada.

Cohen, A. (1969) Custom and Politics in Urban Africa: A Study of Hausa Migrants in Yoruba Towns. London: Routledge and Kegan Paul.

Conseil Attikamek-Montagnais (1979) "Nishastanan Nitasinan (Notre terre nous l'aimons et nous y tenons)." Recherches amérindiennes au Québec 9 (3): 171-182.

Dassetto, F. and A. Bastenier (1988) Europa: nuova frontiera dell'Islaᵣ ι. Rome: Edizioni Lavoro.

De Vos, G. (1975) "Ethnic pluralism: conflict and accommodation," pp. 5-41 in G. De Vos and L. Romanucci-Ross (eds.) Ethnic Identity: Cultural Continuities and Change. Palo Alto, CA: Mayfield.

De Vos, G. (1977) "The passing of passing: ethnic pluralism and the new American society," pp. 220-254 in G. J. Direnzo (ed.) We the people: Social Change. London: Greenwood Press.

De Vos, G., and L. Romanucci-Ross (eds.) (1975) Ethnic Identity: Cultural Continuities and Change. Palo Alto, CA: Mayfield.

Dumon, W. (1985) "De demografische situatie van de vreemdelingen in België," pp. 45-59, in A. Martens and F. Moulaert (eds.) Buitenlandse minderheden in Vlaanderen-België. Antwerp: De Nederlandsche Boekhandel.

Dumon, W. and L. Michiels (1987) OCDE—Système d'observation permanente des migrations, Belgique 1986. Leuven: Institut de Recherches Sociologiques.

Dumont, L. (1980) Homo Hierarchicus: The Caste System and Its Implications. Chicago: University of Chicago Press.

Epstein, A. (1978) Ethos and Identity: Three Studies in Ethnicity. London: Tavistock Publications.

Farley, J. (1982) Majority-Minority Relations. Englewood Cliffs, NJ: Prentice-Hall.

Foyer-stuurgroep bi-cultureel (ed.) (1983) Twee jaar foyer bi-cultureel te Brussel. Een evaluatierapport. Brussels: Foyer.

Frideres, J. (1974) Canada's Indians: Contemporary Conflicts. Scarborough: Prentice-Hall of Canada.

Gagnon, A. (1973) La Baie James indienne. Texte intégral du jugement du juge Albert Malouf. Montreal: Editions du Jour.

Gailly, A. (1983) Een dorp in Turkije. Brussels: Cultuur en Migratie.

Gailly, A and J. Leman (eds.) (1982) Onderwijs, taal- en leermoeilijkheden in de migratie. Leuven: Acco.

Gailly, A., P. Hermans, and J. Leman (1983) Mediterrane dorpsculturen. Brussels: Cultuur en Migratie.

Gans, H. (1979) "Symbolic ethnicity." Ethnic and Racial Studies, 2 (1): 1-20.

Gauvreau, D., F. Bernèche, and J. Fernandez (1982) "La population des Métis et des Indiens sans statut. Essais d'estimation et de distribution spatiale.'' Recherches amérindiennes au Québec, 12 (2): 95–104.

Gendron, G. (1982) "L'alliance laurentienne des Métis et Indiens sans statut inc. Entrevue avec M. Fernand Chalifoux, président, recueillie par G. Gendron." Recherches amérindiennes au Québec, 12 (2): 115–118.

Gérin, L. (1900) La Seigneurie de Sillery et les Hurons de Lorette, Sec. 1, pp. 73–115. Mémoires Société Royale du Canada.

Glazer, N. and D. Moynihan (1963) Beyond the Melting Pot. Cambridge, MA: MIT and Harvard University Press.

Glazer, N. and D. Moynihan (eds.) (1975) Ethnicity: Theory and Experience. Cambridge, MA: Harvard University Press.

Goodenough, W. (1980) Description and Comparison in Cultural Anthropology. London: Cambridge University Press.

Gros-Louis, M. (1981) Le premier des Hurons. Village Huron, Quebec: Réserve indienne.

Gutkind, P. (1974) Urban Anthropology: Perspectives and "Third World" Urbanization and Urbanism. Assen: Van Gorcum.

Hannerz, U. (1976) "Some comments on the anthropology of ethnicity in the United States," pp. 429–438 in Fr. Henry (ed.) Ethnicity in the Americas. Paris: Mouton.

Hargous, S. (1980) Les Indiens du Canada. Tant que l'herbe poussera . . . . Montreal: Presses Sélect.

Heinemeijer, W. F., J. M. M. van Amersfoort, W. Ettema, P. De Mas, and H. H. Van Der Wusten (1977) Partir pour rester: Incidences de l'émigration ouvrière à la campagne marocaine. Amsterdam: Institut Socio-Géographique de l'Université d'Amsterdam.

Heyerick, L. (1985) "Problemen van migrantenkinderen en hun leerkrachten in het Vlaams basisonderwijs," pp. 103–113 in A. Martens and F. Moulaert (eds.) Buitenlandse minderheden in Vlaanderen-België. Antwerp: De Nederlandsche Boekhandel.

Horowitz, D. (1985) Ethnic Groups in Conflict. Berkeley, CA: University of California Press.

Huyse, L. (1981) "Political conflict in bicultural Belgium," pp. 107–126 in A. Lijphart (ed.) Conflict and Coexistence in Belgium: The Dynamics of a Culturally Divided Society. Berkeley, CA: University of California Press.

Jamieson, K. (1978) Indian Women and the Law in Canada: Citizen Minus. Minister of Supply and Services Canada.

Jones, A. (1909) "8endake Ehen" or old Huronia. Toronto.

Kepel, G. (1987) Les banlieues de l'Islam. Naissance d'une religion en France. Paris: Editions du Seuil.

Lemaire, T. (1976) Over de waarde van culturen. Een inleiding in de cultuur-filosofie: Europacentrisme en relativisme. Baarn: Ambo.

Leman, J. (1982) Van Caltanissetta naar Brussel en Genk. Een antropologische studie in de streek van herkomst en in het gastland bij Siciliaanse migranten. Leuven: Acco.

Leman, J. (1984) Integratie, anders bekeken. Brussels: Cultuur en Migratie.

Lévesque, R. (1980) Oui. Montreal: Les éditions de l'Homme.

—LeVine, R. and D. Campbell (1972) Ethnocentrism: Theories of Conflict, Ethnic Attitudes, and Group Behaviour. New York: J. Wiley & Sons.

Lijphart, A. (ed.) (1981) "The Belgian example of cultural coexistence in comparative perspective," pp 1–13 in Conflict and Coexistence in Belgium: The Dynamics of a Culturally Divided Society. Berkeley: University of California Press.

Littlefield, A., L. Lieberman, and L. Reynolds (1982) "Redefining race: the potential demise of a concept in physical anthropology." Current Anthropology, 23 (6): 641–647.

Marangé, J. and A. Lebon (1982) L'insertion des jeunes d'origine étrangère dans la société française. Rapport du Ministre du travail, Président du Haut-Comité de la population et de la famille. Paris: La Documentation française.

Martens, A. (1973) 25 Jaar wegwerparbeiders. Het Belgisch immigratiebeleid na 1945. Leuven: Sociologisch Onderzoeksinstituut.

Martin, C. (1978) Keepers of the Game: Indian–Animal Relationship and the Fur Trade. Berkeley: University of California Press.

Monière, D. (1982) Pour la suite de l'histoire. Essai sur la conjoncture politique au Québec. Montreal: Québec/Amérique.

Morissonneau, C. (1970) "Développement et population de la réserve indienne du Village-Huron, Loretteville." Cahiers de Géographie de Québec, 33: 339–357.

Mukendi wa Meta (1985) L'ethnogenèse luba. Doctoral dissertation. K. U. Leuven: Centre for Social and Cultural Anthropology.

Murdock, G. P. (1959) Africa: Its Peoples and Their Culture History. London: McGraw-Hill.

Owram, D. (1982) "The myth of Louis Riel." The Canadian Historical Review, 63 (3): 315–336.

Patterson, O. (1978) Ethnic Chauvinism: The Reactionary Impulse. New York: Stein and Day.

Pauwels, G. (1983) Dorpen en gemeenschappen in de Andes. Socio-culturele veranderingen bij Boliviaanse Aymara. Leuven: Acco.

Plenel, E. and A. Rollat (1984) "L'effet Le Pen" dossier, La découverte—Le Monde.

Rex, J. and S. Tomlinson (1979) Colonial Immigrants in a British city: A Class Analysis. London: Routledge and Kegan Paul.

Roosens, E. (1971) Socio-culturele verandering in Midden-Afrika. Antwerpen-Utrecht: Standaard Wetenschappelijke Uitgeverij.

Roosens, E. (1979a) Omtrent de achterstelling van immigranten in België. Leuven: Acco.

Roosens, E. (1979b) "Désavantages et discrimination: la question des immigrés en Belgique." EEG-rapport. Rome: Studi Emigrazione, 16 (54): 229–303.

Roosens, E. (1979c) De cultuur van immigrantenkinderen (thema-rapport). Conferentie "Kinderen van Migrerende Werknemers." Rotterdam: Council of the European Communities.

Roosens, E. (1979d) Cultuurverschillen en etnische identiteit. Aspecten van het ontwikkelingsvraagstuk. Brussels: A.B.O.S.

Roosens, E. (1980) "De structuur van een etnisch bewustzijn: de Huronen van Québec," pp. 179–194 in Gedrag, dynamische relatie en betekeniswereld. Leuven: University Press.

Roosens, E. (1981) "The multicultural nature of contemporary Belgian society: the immigrant community," pp. 61–92 in A. Lijphart (ed.) Conflict and Coexistence in Belgium. Berkeley: University of California Press.

Roosens, E. (1982) "Etnische groep en etnische identiteit. Symbolen of concepten?" pp. 99–122 in A. van Amersfoort and H. Entzinger (eds.) Immigrant en samenleving. Deventer: Van Loghum Slaterus.

Roosens, E. (1985) "De sociaal-culturele structuur," pp. 31–44 in A. Martens and F. Moulaert (eds.) Buitenlandse minderheden in Vlaanderen-België. Antwerp: De Nederlandsche Boekhandel.

Roosens, E. (1988) "Migration and caste formation in Europe: the Belgian case." Ethnic and Racial Studies, 11 (2): 207–217.

Rosiers-Leonard, M. C. and J. Polain (1980) Gezamenlijke nota betreffende de situatie in België. Conferentie "Kinderen van Migrerende Werknemers." Rotterdam: Council of the European Communities.

"Sagmai" (1981) "Ouverture d'un centre d'amitié autochtone à Québec." Rencontre, 2 (4): 5.

Sahlins, M. (1976) Culture and Practical Reason. Chicago: University of Chicago Press.

Salmon, P. (1973) Le racisme devant l'histoire. Paris/Brussels: Nathan-Labor.

Savard, R. and J.-R. Proulx (1982) Canada. Derrière l'épopée, les autochtones. Montreal: L'Hexagone.

Schwartz, T. (1976) "The cargo cult: A Melanesian type response to change," pp. 157–206 in G. De Vos (ed.) Responses to Change: Society, Culture and Personality. New York: Van Nostrand.

Thernstrom, S. (1980) Harvard Encyclopedia of American Ethnic Groups. Cambridge, MA: The Belknapp Press of Harvard University Press.

Thränhardt, D. (1985) " 'Buitenlanders' als voorwerp van Duitse ideologische belangen en ideologieën," pp. 289–305 in A. Martens and F. Moulaert (eds.) Buitenlandse minderheden in Vlaanderen-België. Antwerp: De Nederlandsche Boekhandel.

Tooker, E. (1964) An ethnography of the Huron Indians, 1615–1649. Bureau of American Ethnology Bulletin 190. Washington, D.C.

Trigger, B. (1976) The Children of Aataentsic: A History of the Huron People to 1660. Montreal–London: McGill and Queen's University Presses.

van den Berg-Eldering, L., F. de Rijcke, and L. Zuck (eds.) (1983) Multicultural Education. Dordrecht: Foris Publications.

Vansina, J. (1971) Cultures et développement, 3 (4): 826–828.

Vincent, M. (1978) "Un siècle de réclamations de la Seigneurie de Sillery par les Hurons (1791–1896)." Recherches amérindiennes au Québec, 7: 21–22.

About the Author

Eugeen E. Roosens is Professor and Head of the Department of Anthropology at the Catholic University of Leuven, Belgium. He has taught at Leuven since 1965 and has also taught at universities in the United States, Canada, and Zaire. He is appointed P. P. Rubens Professor at the University of California, Berkeley, for the academic year 1989–1990. Dr. Roosens has done fieldwork among the Yaka in Zaire, with the Huron Indians in Quebec, and in Geel, Belgium. Since 1974 he has directed the project "The Cultural Identity of Ethnic Minorities," a long-term fieldwork project by a team of scholars which operates in five continents. This book is an outgrowth of that project. Dr. Roosens also directed the anthropological team for the Gee! project, which concerned the community placement of the mentally ill in a Belgian town. His book on Geel has been translated into English, French, German, and Japanese. Dr. Roosens has written half a dozen other books and research monographs on Africa, ethnicity, and immigration questions.